Get It
Set It
Move It
Prove It

60 Ways to Get Real Results In Your Organization

Mark Graham Brown

Productivity *Press*

NEW YORK

Most Productivity Press books are available at quantity discounts when
purchased in bulk. For more information contact our Customer Service
Department (888-319-5852). Address all other inquires to:

Productivity Press
444 Park Avenue South, 7th floor
New York, NY 10016
United States of America
Telephone 212-686-5900
Fax: 212-686-5411
E-mail: info@productivitypress.com

Composition by William H. Brunson Typography Services
Proofreading by Mary A. Junewick
Printed and bound by Malloy Litho in the United States of America

Library of Congress Cataloging-in-Publication Data

Brown, Mark Graham.
    Get it, set it, move it, prove it : 60 ways to get real results in your
organization / Mark Graham Brown.
        p. cm.
    Includes bibliographical references and index.
    ISBN 1-56327-306-3 (alk. paper)
    1. Industrial management.   2. Business planning.   I. Title: 60
ways to get real results in your organization.   II. Title.
HD31.B7657 2004
658.4—dc22

                                                              2004016709

08   07   8   7   6   5   4   3   2

Dedication

This book is dedicated to a couple of guys who served as my mentors during the years and have had a profound impact on my life. Dr. Richard Malott and Larry Short. Dr. Malott is an author, publisher, professor, and a competent rock & roll drummer. He was my advisor in graduate school and taught me two very valuable skills I have used throughout my career: writing and public speaking. Larry Short is the former president of Creative Universal, my first employer. Larry taught me about business and values, and that it is possible to be a successful business person and have a lot of fun while getting the work done.

Contents

Introduction

This book is for anyone who wants to produce real results in a job or organization. Real results don't necessarily mean profits. Real results are *outcomes*—such as healthier people, better-educated children, improved market share, happier customers who buy more of your stuff, and happier employees who would never think of leaving to work for a competitor. This book is for senior executives and individual contributors, and anyone in between. It provides practical and useful suggestions on things you can start doing *now* to improve performance, and things you should avoid or stop doing as soon as possible.

Everyone Wants a Quick Fix

The popularity of diet books, exercise equipment sold via infomercials, and liposuction attests to the fact that people are always looking for a new and easier way of accomplishing their goals. Seven or eight years ago fat was the enemy, and food companies scrambled to come up with low-fat everything, from muffins to peanut butter. Now, no one seems to care about fat grams—carbohydrates, or carbs, are the new evil. Now there is low-carb beer and even low-carb bread. Does the South Beach or Atkins diet work any better than the diets of ten years ago that focused on low-fat foods? Who knows? But people are always searching for some new approach that will be easier, cheaper, and require less effort than the old one.

We do this in our personal lives and we do this at work. It is human nature to try to find the easiest and cheapest solution to our problems, or the easiest way of accomplishing our goals. Some slick consultant with impressive credentials comes along with a new program, which many admired companies have already purchased, and it is tempting to jump on the bandwagon rather than be left in the dust.

Beware of Management Fads

As you begin to read this book, you might be offended or put off by the fact that I am not a big fan of some program or initiative that your organization is currently enamored with. I am not against anything that works. What I am against is wasting time and money on programs that often fail to produce real improvements in performance.

It never ceases to amaze me to see the way organizations continue to waste money and time on things that do not work: new products that no one buys; changes to products that were fine before they were messed with; projects, programs, initiatives, and all kinds of strategies that suck company coffers dry. Over the years, we have seen many management initiatives, such as:

1. Management by objectives
2. Strategic planning
3. Activity-based costing
4. Total quality management
5. Integrated product development
6. Quality function deployment
7. Reengineering
8. Six sigma
9. Lean manufacturing
10. Balanced scorecard
11. Customer relationship management

Some of these programs are still very much a part of many organizations, and some have kind of disappeared or morphed into something with a new name. Although all of these programs have been successful in some organizations, many organizations dropped them before they had a chance to reap the benefits and went off in search for something newer and easier.

The Baldrige Award Model Has Weathered the Storm

One system that has endured over at least the last fifteen years is the criteria for the Malcolm Baldrige Award. What started out as an

award geared for manufacturing companies with good quality programs has evolved into a set of guidelines for assessing the health
of any business, government, health care, or educational organization. The Baldrige model has become the standard, not only in the
United States but in most countries around the world, for identifying a well-run organization. The U.S. government has found that
winners of the Baldrige Award, which are publicly traded companies, significantly outperformed (i.e., three to four times better) the
stock market in eight of the last nine years. This is better performance than most mutual funds you can buy.

One of the reasons the Baldrige model has endured and grown
in acceptance over fifteen years is that it has been mostly immune to
management fads. The criteria never ask about your e-business
strategy, six-sigma effort, or balanced scorecard. The Baldrige
model has remained nondenominational and accepting of a wide
variety of programs and approaches, as long as they work for your
organization. There is no one recipe for running a good organization. There are many different formulas and approaches, but the
core systems should always be in place to drive performance. The
Baldrige model is about those core systems, which should be found
in all types and sizes of organizations.

Problems with The Baldrige Model

There are a number of problems with the Baldrige model, however. First of all, it has not been marketed well, and many people
I run into have never heard of the award or the criteria. The government has done a terrible job of marketing the criteria to organizations that could benefit from following the model. If you
interviewed one hundred people at any mall in America and asked
them what the Baldrige Award was, probably ten out of one hundred would have heard of it. Of those ten, probably eight are mis-
informed as to the criteria on which the award is based. Many
think that the award is about quality, or what used to be called total
quality management. It was about quality in the beginning, but any
reference to quality, or TQM, was stripped out of the criteria

almost ten years ago. Since 1995, the Baldrige model has been about all aspects of performance—quality, profitability, customer satisfaction, employee satisfaction, and meeting regulatory and other stakeholder requirements.

Aside from being poorly marketed, a bigger problem with the award criteria is that they are incredibly complicated and poorly written. Each year the criteria get more complicated; more points, subpoints, and sub-subpoints are added, so you need a team of ten Ph.D.s to try to decipher them. I wrote the first book on how to interpret the Baldrige Award criteria. *Baldrige Award Winning Quality* is currently in its 13th edition and continues to sell well. It is quite long and still fairly technical, with more information than needed by the average executive or employee. Consequently, in 1994, I wrote a new book called *The Pocket Guide to the Baldrige Award Criteria*. This little sixty-page book is written at about an eighth-grade reading level and is tailored for the average person who needs a general understanding of how the award criteria work. It outsells the big one by a huge margin, but I still think it misses the mark for a lot of people.

Quit Teaching the Model or Come Up with a Better One

I started working with the state of Washington a few years ago, and I would say it, along with South Carolina, is a leader in applying the Baldrige criteria to the running of state government. At a presentation a few years ago, I heard a talk by one of the Washington state leaders who said he had given up trying to teach the Baldrige model to employees. He explained:

> We trained them and trained them, used simple language, translated the criteria into terms relevant to state government, and found that most of them still did not get it. Most employees, from workers to senior managers, struggled with how to apply this complicated systems model to running their day-to-day operation. So we gave up and no longer teach the

Baldrige model or even mention it. What we teach them now is how to get results. The techniques we teach are the same things embedded in the Baldrige model, like figuring out who your customers are and what they want, but we don't teach Baldrige and we find that employees do just fine without understanding the conceptual model behind the way we want to run state government.

This presentation was a great revelation to me. I have made a career and written two books on how to understand this outstanding but complicated model. Yet what people really need to know is how to apply the principles of the Baldrige model in their school, company, department, or unit. What they also need to know is how to avoid time-wasting initiatives and programs that have good surface credibility but actually do little to produce real results.

This book is about how to get real results and be able to *prove it* (which is the theme of Part IV of this book). For the last twenty-five years, I have worked as a consultant to many of the Fortune 50, all branches of the U.S. military, many state and federal government organizations, and companies in fifteen other countries. Over the years, I've seen a lot of stupid time-wasting activities and a lot of things that really worked. This book is about things that have really worked and how to avoid the things that I've found mostly don't work. I needed a way to organize my thoughts, so I sorted my ideas and suggestions into a conceptual model I call:

Get it
Set it
Move it
Prove it

Here's how the framework of this book corresponds to the Baldrige criteria:

❏ The *Get It* part of the Baldrige criteria asks about your leadership vision and values (Part 1.1 of Baldrige), your customers and their needs (Part 3.1 of Baldrige), and your strategy.

❏ The *Set It* portion of the criteria asks about your goals and strategies in the areas of ethics and meeting regulatory requirements (Part 1.2 of Baldrige), your goals and how they are deployed (Part 2.2 of Baldrige), the measures of performance used to manage the organization (Part 4.1 of Baldrige), and your system for communicating performance information (Part 4.2 of Baldrige).

❏ The *Move It* portion of the Baldrige criteria asks about how you build relationships with important customers (Part 3.2 of Baldrige); how you select, train, and manage your employees (Part 5 of Baldrige, the human resource focus); and how you mange your key work processes (Part 6 of Baldrige, on process management) to ensure consistency and efficiency.

❏ Finally, *Prove It* corresponds to the last section in the Baldrige criteria (Part 7, on business results), which is worth almost half the points. It is about proving that your approaches and systems really work to produce high performance in your results.

Get It

What I've done is essentially simplified the Baldrige model into a four-stage approach that uses simple and easy-to-remember terms. The Baldrige model is about *getting it*, or figuring out your mission, who you exist to serve (i.e., customers), what people want and expect, and what your organization stands for. The "getting it" part of the model is all about figuring things out.

Sadly, there are a number of organizations out there that do not seem to *get it*. Hence, the first part of the book is about all the things an organization needs to figure out to be successful. A lot of this stuff may sound like common sense, but common sense is not all that common in many organizations. If you don't *get it*, you will have little success with the other parts of the model, and I run into a number of organizations with gaping holes in their approach to figuring out what they need to do to be successful. In other words, they just don't *get it*.

Set It

Once you have figured out all the important pieces of information you need to have a solid organization, you need to set a course for the future. This involves *setting* your direction by creating a vision, goals, measurements, and strategies for achieving the goals.

Sadly, many organizations are not very good at this stuff. They all have binders or brochures called strategic plans, but many of those plans are done so poorly that they are laughable. Vision statements look like they were written by Dilbert, goals are generic and not well researched, targets are made up out of thin air, and strategies are selected that are based more on politics than any real research. Yes, most organizations have all the components of a plan and scorecard, but most also miss the mark by a long shot.

This second section of the book is about how to properly *set* your future direction and how to avoid some of the time-wasting activities I've seen in too many otherwise well-run organizations. How can the organization be successful if the plan is so bad? No one pays much attention to it once it is written and revised. Employees go back to doing real work that produces important outcomes. Planning and measuring performance are important for all types and sizes of organizations. However, a poorly written plan is unlikely to be well executed, or even read and remembered.

Move It

The first two parts of the book are about doing things that don't generate revenue. Market research, planning, and measuring performance are not what most people consider real work. Real work is stuff like cooking food in a restaurant, framing a house, fixing a car, debugging software, or delivering a package. *Moving it* is about *performance*. It is about doing the things that your organization exists for. Yes, a school needs to understand its customers, mission, vision, and so forth. But more important, the school needs to teach the students what they need to know.

Moving it also means moving the needles on your dashboard or scorecard to demonstrate real results. Most of the people and other resources are devoted to the *move it* activities because this is the real work. It is rare to find an organization that is completely incompetent at the main thing it does. An airline that is always late and provides horrible service is quickly bankrupt. A restaurant with bad food and service closes its door in a couple of months. There are severe consequences to not being very good at the *move it* stuff.

Organizations get into trouble in this phase of the model when they get big enough to have a bunch of staff or corporate types who try to improve how they *move it*. In other words, they try to implement programs and approaches to save money, improve efficiency, or improve the quality of the work done by those "moving it." These consultants and corporate types try all kinds of things to get better performance from front-line workers: training programs, better tools, team meetings, new software, rewards, and all sorts of other programs, initiatives, and projects designed to get more work for less cost. The third section of the book will tell you more things to avoid than good things to do, but there are a few chapters that provide suggestions of good practices I have seen.

Prove It

The fourth section of the book asks the question, "So what?" What if you did all the things I advised you to do in the first three parts of the book and avoided all the stupid stuff I told you to avoid? The test of any action or effort is results. Did the drug take away your headache? Did the new sales proposal get you the deal? Did the new bonus program produce real improvements in employee performance? *Proving it* is about results, outcomes, or performance.

The first three parts of this book are about activities, behavior, strategies, and things to do. The last part of the book is about how to look at the right numbers to really prove to yourself and others that your strategies and approaches do work.

Proving it is about data, graphs, numbers, and how to make sense out of all those numbers that organizations collect and report. You will find chapters in this section about ensuring that you are looking at the right statistics, as well as how to analyze the data to determine the next course of action. This is not a book on accounting or statistics. What you will find in this section are basic suggestions on how to really *prove* that your outcomes have improved and that your goals have been achieved. If the numbers show that you have fallen short, the problem lies somewhere else in the model, and you need to loop back to the *Get it* phase and start working through the model again until you can *prove* that you have achieved your goals.

Acknowledgments

Jim Stuart of Franklin Covey, along with Lisa Downey-Hood and Rick Fuller of the Norfolk Naval Shipyard, originally conceived the idea for this book and the title. The four of us worked together many projects at the shipyard, and I am grateful for the opportunity to have worked with such innovative and competent individuals. I also thank them for allowing me to take their *Get it*, *Set it*, *Move it*, *Prove it* model and turn it into a book.

GET IT

SET IT

MOVE IT

PROVE IT

Know What's Important

Have you ever done business with an organization that just doesn't *get it*? Have you ever worked for a boss that just doesn't *get it*? There seem to be a lot of organizations that are clueless when it comes to meeting even the most basic customer requirements. There seem to be a number of executives out there who are clueless as to what employees or customers want and expect. They understand what shareholders want. That's easy: good earnings. What they don't seem to understand is customers, employees, suppliers, and others.

This first part of the book is about *getting it*. The focus of this first set of chapters is leadership and defining the requirements of customers and other stakeholders. At the most basic level, *getting it* is about defining why your organization even exists. Some organizations I've worked with don't even get this. Their mission statement is so convoluted and characterized by a litany of buzz words, that it is hard to tell what they really do and why they exist.

The chapters that follow are a mix of advice and stories about what to do and what not to do. There are examples of some of the best practices I've seen relating to *getting it*, as well as some of the dumber things I've seen that you can hopefully avoid.

Thankfully, there are a few organizations out there that really do *get it*. Those that do tend to have the following characteristics. Organizations that *get it* have:

- Clearly defined the reasons for their existence, or their mission
- Defined a well thought-out set of values that they actually live by
- Carefully selected each individual leader
- Used creative techniques to figure out what customers really want
- Accurately identified their weaknesses and limitations
- Learned their core competencies

- Been careful to continue doing the things that made them successful
- Always been aware of major and minor competitive threats
- Watched what's going on in the world to determine how it might affect them
- Made it as easy as possible for customers to buy their products or services
- Stuck to promises made to customers, employees, and others

In short, organizations that *get it* are the ones that lead their markets and leave their competitors scratching their heads and trying to catch up.

Forget Focus Groups and Surveys for Market Research

Asking customers what they want via focus groups and surveys are the most common ways of figuring out how to design a new product or service that will really sell. This approach looks very scientific but rarely produces results that matter. The first problem is that people are not very good at predicting their future behavior. Somebody shows us something, we think it looks pretty cool and works pretty well, and we tell the market researcher that we would buy it. We rarely do, however. What we say we are going to do and what we really do are often quite different. Perhaps we want to make the market research person feel good, or we just aren't very good at defining what is important to us.

For example, one well-known fast-food restaurant chain has spent a lot of money on market research over the last few years to try to improve its shrinking sales and market share. People told them that if they had healthier choices of food they would come to the restaurants more often. Some said they wanted better salads, but most said they wanted fewer calories and lower-fat versions of hamburgers, fries, and shakes. So this restaurant's chefs went to work and created a lean hamburger that was about one-third lower in calories and fat than the typical fast-food burger, and those who tasted it in focus groups all thought it was amazingly good for a low-fat burger. As the fast-food chain tested it out on the menu of a few restaurants, more and more people tried it, really liked it, and said they would buy it, so the chain introduced it in all its restaurants and promoted it in its advertising.

No one bought it. Everyone said they wanted low-fat and low-calorie choices, but the biggest sellers in this and other fast-food restaurants are super-size items like an extra three pounds of french fries for fifty cents more. People don't like to admit they are pigs. They especially don't want to admit that in a focus group meeting, so they gave this fast-food restaurant a politically correct answer—that they were concerned about calories and fat. Given that about two-thirds of America is overweight, it does not look like too many people are that concerned about eating low-calorie food. This fast-food chain made the mistake of believing what people told them they wanted. People go to fast-food restaurants looking for grease, salt, and kids' toys, not low-calorie food. Afraid of lawsuits and bad press, this chain has now taken the lead in removing the giant-size choices from its menu before someone successfully sues a fast-food chain for making them obese.

Many smart companies have made the mistake of believing market research studies based on asking people what they want. People either don't know what they want, or lie. Focus groups and surveys are notoriously unreliable methods of determining customer needs and requirements.

Momentum Textiles in Irvine, California, designs and sells fabrics for commercial applications in restaurants, hotels, offices, and other types of facilities. They tried focus groups and surveys to test out new fabric designs, and the ones the focus groups picked never sold well. Momentum has since stopped doing these formal focus group meetings where people vote on their favorite fabrics. Instead, they bring designs and samples to meetings with architects and designers, and watch their behavior. Which fabric they pick up first and how long they hold it is always a clue, Momentum's sales manager recently told me. He explained that they have learned to watch customers' eyes, hands, smiles, and other subtle cues to tell them what is going to be a hot seller and which fabrics are not going to sell.

Since Momentum adopted this approach its sales have skyrocketed, and it has excelled at selecting fabrics that really sell. Sales and marketing folks in the company tell me that 2003 was their best year to date while their competitors have all had declining sales due to the sagging economy.

How to Get It: Know What's Important

A huge part of *getting it* is figuring out what is important to your customers and what they want. Traditional market research is supposed to help organizations figure this out. Unfortunately, many companies that don't *get it* keep turning out the stuff people *said* they wanted but that no one seems to buy.

Smart organizations that *get it* have found innovative and creative ways of figuring out what turns people on and what they are likely to buy in the future. Here's how to *get it*:

❑ ***Don't rely on focus groups, whose members aren't always truthful—even if they intend to be.*** Many people just aren't comfortable confessing their true buying habits.

❑ ***Do get out in the field and observe what your customers are actually buying***, and watch firsthand how they make their buying decisions. Find out what characteristics of your products or services are most appealing to your customers, and then focus on those characteristics.

Develop Some Real Values and Stick to Them

Enron, WorldCom, HealthSouth, Adelphia, Arthur Andersen, and every other company that has gotten into major problems because of unethical behavior had a set of values and code of ethics. In fact, those codes probably sound just like the trite and unimaginative list of vague words that you have in your own lobby:

Trust	Integrity	Diversity
Customer Satisfaction	Honesty	Innovation
Teamwork	Respect	Excellence

Organizations that *get it* put some thought into the type of culture they want to have, and work hard to maintain it as the organization grows and changes, and leaders come and go. The job of leadership is to define the values and ensure that everyone models them in their behavior—especially the bosses.

Well-run organizations develop a unique culture that is impervious to changes in leadership. Southwest Airlines' culture of hard work mixed with lots of laughter did not change a bit when founder and former CEO Herb Kelleher retired. They all miss Herb, and the new boss is not quite the colorful character that Herb is, but the culture of Southwest endures, and it remains one of the most admired companies.

My first boss built a company that had the same type of strong culture. Creative Universal President Larry Short taught us all three priorities:

- Always give the client more than he or she expects.
- None of us is as smart as all of us.
- Let's have fun while getting it done.

7

G
E
T

I
T

These values permeated this small consulting and training firm of 200 people, and we always kept Larry's values in our heads. We got lots of repeat work from happy clients and had a lot of fantastic parties. Sadly, a big corporation bought Creative Universal. Larry left, as did I and many of the other fun, hardworking people, and the culture was never the same. Larry Short ensured that these values permeated the culture of his small company through communication and his own behavior. In case we forgot our three values, there were signs and reminders everywhere, and Larry modeled these values in all of his actions and decisions. I remember many instances when he decided to lose money on a project in order to ensure that the client was happy. Larry modeled the teamwork value by not having a desk in his office. Rather, he had a round table where four to six people could sit to discuss things that came up, and he always had people in his office. Finally, Larry threw some great parties and seemed to have more fun at them than just about any other employee—he loved parties.

How to Get It: Know What's Important

A set of values and a culture is much easier in a company of 200 than a company of 50,000 employees, but it is still possible with a good plan and continued attention to maintaining the culture. An organization needs a set of values that are clearly understood by all employees. You cannot write rules for every situation, and the values should guide your behavior and help you decide what's the right thing to do. Here's how to *get it*:

❑ **Don't just copy the same list of values** everyone else has and print them on employee badges.

❑ **Do create a realistic set of values** that really defines the way your organization operates. Then monitor the behavior and decisions of all your employees against those values to ensure that they are upheld.

Learn What You Can Be Good at and Stick to It

A key to success in any endeavor is figuring out what you can be good at and continuing to do those one or two things at which you excel. We all had to learn that as individuals, and organizations need to learn that lesson as well. Some call this defining your mission or core competencies. This means identifying what your core business is and writing a statement that defines exactly what you do, why you exist, and, hopefully, keeps you focused on doing the things that made you successful in the first place.

Organizations that *get it* stay very focused and do not change their mission unless there is a solid business reason for doing so. Often, the pressure for growth in earnings causes companies to do stupid things. When you stray too far from the things you are good at you not only fail at the new thing, but the failure sometimes causes you to fail at the one thing you were good at because all of your attention is focused on the new stuff. A prime example of an organization that does not *get it* is Sears.

Sears has a long history of being one of the most successful companies in America. Sears is a trusted brand name and a store in which many Americans have shopped. For many people, a Sears credit card was their first one. Sears grew to become the biggest and most respected department store in the country, but then it began expanding its business into other areas. It leveraged its strong brand name by selling rental cars (Budget), insurance (Allstate), credit cards (Discover) and financial services (Dean Witter). As the company was growing more diverse, its core department store business began to falter. In 1995, the company had a net loss, and a new CEO was appointed to reverse Sears's declining performance (*Harvard Business Review*, January/February 1998).

While Sears was expanding into other nonretail business, its department stores started to decline. I believe that many formerly loyal customers started going to Target, Home Depot, Macy's, and other stores for the majority of their shopping. Sears decided to refocus attention on retail again and sold off Discover Card, Allstate, Budget, and Dean Witter. It returned to its original mission of being the biggest and best department store. But it had lost a good number of its previously loyal customers and has been unable to win many of them back. Sears has tried to sell appliances through a Web site (Sears.com) that is now defunct. Sears Homelife Furniture stores are gone, and Sears hardware stores can't seem to compete with Loew's and Home Depot. It recently sold its credit card business to Citigroup for $32 billion. It keeps selling stuff to stay afloat—and spending the money on failed business ventures. Is Sears a company that still does not *get it*? I think so.

Jim Collins calls this focus on what you can be good at "the hedgehog principle." The nearly blind hedgehog accomplishes his digging by relentlessly focusing on his goal. It is possible to keep focusing on a product or service for which there is no longer a market, and part of *getting it* is being in touch with the marketplace and adjusting your mission when necessary.

Sometimes straying from your core mission even a little is dangerous. The largest and most successful beer company in the USA, Anheuser Busch, decided a few years ago to get into the potato chip and pretzel business, which sounded like a perfect fit for a beer company, since many of the same core competencies would be needed. The snack company did okay, but I believe it never produced the kind of results Anheuser Busch was hoping for, and it learned that making and selling snacks was different from making and selling beer. Anheuser Busch is now back to doing one thing that it does exceptionally well—making beer. Straying from your mission even a little can be a risk.

**G
E
T

I

T**

How to Get It: Know What's Important

Big organizations sometimes get too cocky and think they can be good at any business—they usually can't. Those that *get it* know what they are good at and continue doing those things that made them successful in the first place. Here's how to *get it*:

❏ ***Don't lose focus and stray too far from your core business, even if you branch out into seemingly related businesses.***

❏ ***Do define your mission clearly, in plain English, and stay focused on that mission.*** As long as your product or service continues to fill a real need for people, keep doing what you're doing well.

Don't Underestimate
the Competition

One of the problems with success is that you start to believe you are invincible. It happens to people, and it happens to organizations. A big part of *getting it* is realizing that no organization is invincible. Sears thought it was invincible and didn't pay much attention to Wal-Mart, Target, and Home Depot until they came along and took away its customers. General Motors didn't see Toyota as much of a threat until Toyota took a big chunk of GM's market share. French wineries dominated the market for years and did not see California wines as a serious threat until a major chunk of their market had been eroded. Years later, California wineries are hopefully worried about competitors in Australia, Chile, and other places that are producing some excellent wines.

How about Microsoft? Do you think it's worried at all about other software companies? I hope it is. No matter how big and how successful you are, some unknown competitor can ambush you and steal your business with a better product or service at a cheaper price. United, Delta, and American Airlines pretty much owned the market for business travel. Given that an airline makes close to 80 percent of its profit from business flyers, the big airlines were not concerned about companies like Southwest and Jet Blue. A few years later, both United and American are on the verge of bankruptcy and Southwest and Jet Blue are profitable and growing.

Every year we hear stories about big companies that just don't *get it*. They seem to be a victim of their own success and are unable to see that a business model that worked in the past may no longer be viable. The record industry is one that does not seem to *get it* these days. Music sales continue to decline as more and more people refuse to pay $15 for a CD that has maybe two good songs on it. Instead, they download the two good songs from the Internet, and put them on a blank CD for which they paid 25 cents. The entire business model of selling CDs through music and department stores is not working like it used to. One record company has started lowering prices on CDs to $10, but most people I talk to think this is still too much. So, rather than change the business model and distribution system, record companies are trying to sue children who download songs for copyright violation to stop the piracy. Stealing someone's copyrighted material is clearly wrong, but this industry does not seem to *get it*. Rather than looking at the Internet as a low-cost distribution network for music, record companies view it as a tool for stealing their product that must be stopped.

The competitors you need to be concerned about are probably the ones you don't know about. Barnes and Noble was watching Walden and Borders but didn't see Amazon.com as much of a threat until it was too late. Often, these edge competitors are small companies that have taken a different approach or adopted a different business model. If you wait until the new business model is proven successful, it will be too late to copy it. United tried to copy Southwest ten years ago by forming a new business unit called United Shuttle that offered the same fares, schedules, and every other aspect of Southwest's strategy. But it could not copy the culture of Southwest, so United Shuttle is now out of business while Southwest continues to flourish. United has now resurrected the old concept of United Shuttle with a new airline called Ted. I guess it is short for united—cute. I've yet to take a flight on Ted, and I doubt that Southwest is too worried about it.

GET IT

How to Get It: Know What's Important

Leading companies that *get it* are those that are always watching the competition. Many great companies have come and gone in the last fifty years, and those that disappeared were often those that did not see competitive threats until it was too late. Here's how to *get it*:

❑ ***Don't view your company as invincible—and don't overlook any potential competitors.*** To be on the safe side, it is wise to always overestimate the threat faced from competitors. Assume the enemy will put you out of business someday unless you launch an offensive strike. Being a little more careful and a little more worried than you should be is a good thing, though it's hard to do when you're the biggest cat in the jungle. Nevertheless, no matter how large or small your company is, you need to be constantly aware of who's competing for your customer.

❑ ***Do continual market and competitive research.*** If you want your organization to be one of the few that does *get it*, you need to dedicate people to studying current and potential competitors. And you need to convince executives of the real threats that exist before it is too late.

Eat Your Own Dog Food

Executives that don't *get it* are those who fail to appreciate what customers and employees must go through to do business with their firm. Companies that *get it* are those that regularly have leaders experience what customers experience or work in the front line of a customer service job. Forward-thinking airline executives book their own tickets and fly coach across country to see what customers really experience. Of course, the flight attendants and pilots are often tipped off so the executives get an unrealistic view of reality, but the smart ones go incognito so they can really experience what the customer experiences.

Experiencing your own products and services through the eyes of a customer is a great way of finding out how good or bad your organization is. It is also a good way to do market research and learn what is important to customers. The six-foot, four-inch executive who has to fly in a coach seat for three hours learns very quickly the importance of an extra six inches of leg room.

Leaders often get a completely unrealistic view of their organizations when they sample the company products or services. My friend Steve is an executive in a chain of Italian and French restaurants. When Steve walks into any of his company restaurants they have already been warned that he is coming, the manager greets him at the door with his favorite drink, he is escorted to the best table in the place, and the best looking waitress brings him an appetizer. The chef comes out to shake his hand, waiters and waitresses smile at him and make him feel welcome, and overall he is treated like a king. Steve samples his restaurants' food and service on a regular basis, but he is not seeing reality.

Steve's restaurants have wonderful atmosphere, great food, and excellent service, so it was a treat to go there—not anything that could be construed as work. His previous employer owned a large chain of low-priced restaurants slightly nicer than Denny's, but not much nicer. The executives in this company entertained a lot and never went to their own restaurants. They wouldn't be caught dead eating the slop that they made their customer eat. These guys were big-shot executives and would only visit the restaurants on occasional announced inspections. To even have lunch in one of their own restaurants truly was work. Of course, whenever they visited a restaurant, the staff polished and cleaned everything the night before to make sure the bosses were pleased at how spotless and well run the place was. These executives didn't *get it* either. They did not see what their customers had to experience.

Part of *getting it* is seeing life through the eyes of front-line employees as well as through your customers' eyes. HMO PacifiCare regularly has executives man the phones in the customer service department so they can see how tough it is talking all day long to customers who are mostly calling to present questions or problems. Executives in PacifiCare experience the frustration of customers this way, as well as the frustration of customer service reps who take the heat for health care providers, claims, and other people not doing their job. When I worked with PacifiCare years ago, this effort, which it called keeping in touch, was done on a quarterly basis by all company executives, and it really helped them stay in touch with the employees and the customers.

How to Get It: Know What's Important

Companies that *get it* know firsthand what their customers are getting. Their top executives, managers, and employees have walked a mile in their customers' shoes to find out what problems customers face and how their company solves them. Here's how to *get it*:

❑ ***Don't fall into the trap of thinking that you are better than your customers.*** If you have no interest in using the products your company makes or sells or the services your company provides, then you're in the wrong business. And you should get out before you run it into the ground.

❑ ***Do put yourself in your customer's place.*** Call your own customer service line and find out how long you have to wait for help and how friendly the reception is when the service rep comes on the line. Order one of your products and see how quickly and in what condition it arrives. When you test your own products and services, your customers and your company benefit.

6

Find Out What Aggravates Customers

Organizations spend a lot of money trying to find ways to delight us. Extra miles, extra soaps, fancy packaging, no-cost options, free minutes, free months, and other things are supposed to entice us to buy and continue to buy their products and services. When we do buy, what we want is something pretty basic, and most of us are not thrilled by these little extras. What we want more than anything else is to have a product or service work like it is supposed to and not be aggravated when we are buying it or trying to enjoy it. How many aggravations do you think today's airline passengers have to put up with to go from point A to point B? Try contacting your local motor vehicle department for anything more than a routine transaction and see how many aggravations you must endure. Try taking something back to a discount retail store and it will make you think twice about shopping there again. For that matter, try buying stuff at one of these places on a Saturday. They even make spending money a pain in the butt.

Organizations would do better if they figured out all the little and big things they do to aggravate us and then eliminate them, rather than waste time trying to "delight" us with extras when they can't even get the basics right. Forget the espresso in the service department of the car dealership, just get my car fixed right when you promised. Forget the extra miles and certificates for free trips that always seem to come with a page of restrictions that make them unusable, just get the planes to land safely and on time. Forget sending your friendly account reps on monthly visits with more samples

18

of drugs that have two pages of side effects and don't seem to work for many patients, try to market a drug that works without having side effects that are worse than the symptoms being treated.

Ever try to buy anything on the Internet? Most sites are so complicated and have so many screens where you have to enter your e-mail address and password that it is almost less aggravating to contact your call center and wait on hold for twenty minutes.

How about shopping at a home-improvement superstore on Saturday? Whenever I've shopped at one of these retailers on the weekend, I always have to park my car half a mile away; I get lost trying to find the items I came for; I try to find a store employee to help me and eventually give up, but not before filling my cart with a bunch of stuff that I didn't even intend to buy. Then I wait in line with a bunch of other weekend warriors; I finally see a store employee, but he is not there to help me. Instead, he wants to check my bags and receipt to make sure I didn't steal anything. Selection and savings are important, and the superstores excel at both, but I think they could make shopping a little less aggravating.

Some leading organizations, such as FedEx, have done a lot of research on the different things they can do to aggravate a customer. They not only have a long list of these aggravations, they rank them from the most minor to the worst. If your package was on the plane with Tom Hanks in *Castaway*, that would probably qualify as a Level 10 aggravation. Leading organizations know all the ways they can make life difficult for customers and not only measure the occurrence of these things, they try to eliminate the aggravations entirely. Returning a rental car is now rarely aggravating thanks to hand-held terminals that agents use to check you in and get you a receipt. However, cashing a check at a bank is still, at best, a minor aggravation.

How to Get It: Know What's Important

❏ *Don't try to delight your customers.* Just do your job and make it easy for them to spend money on your product or service.

❏ *Do find out the things that drive us crazy and STOP DOING THEM!* Companies that *get* this simple concept are the ones that continue to capture our business.

E
T
I
T

Stop Lying to Customers, Employees, and Shareholders

The world is in an ethics crisis. We never really trusted politicians, and learned years ago that they tell all sorts of lies to get elected and stay in office. It has pretty much been accepted that we don't expect them to be honest. In the last few years, we've learned that pretty much anybody in a position of power is a liar—our executives, our teachers, our priests, our doctors. In 2000, a study by KPMG LLP on organizational integrity revealed that only 23 percent of of people trust corporate executives these days. The only group trusted less was used car salespeople (15 percent).

Some of us have become so jaded that we assume we are being lied to unless proven otherwise. Honesty has become such a rare thing that when we encounter it, it is refreshing. Perhaps calling yourself the honest corporation would be a viable business strategy. But if a company had that as its slogan, we wouldn't believe it anyway. I guess that's why you see so many "Honest Dan's," "Honest Jim's," and "Honest Bill's" used car lots. In an industry known to be rife with dishonesty, some have tried to separate themselves from the pack by professing their honesty.

Why is there so much lying going on? First of all, there is a lot of pressure to produce good results. Shareholders, boards, regulators, and others are all pushing for performance and compliance. But the pressure's always been there, and the economy has been through many up and down periods. I think two of the biggest reasons is that lying has become so commonplace now is that we

21

**G
E
T

I
T**

rationalize it and call it spin. The spin doctors can take a situation or fact and twist it around so that a negative situation becomes a "positive" one. Public relations specialists have gotten really good at presenting things in a positive light, even though the ship is sinking.

Honesty is a value on the wall of most big companies, including most of those that have gotten into trouble for lying. We all believe honesty is important, but not many practice it.

The second reason lying has become so prevalent is that we get away with it. To some parents lying about something you did wrong was worse than the act itself. Many parents try to impress the importance of honesty on kids at an early age by rewarding them for honesty and punishing them for lying. As adults we learn that we can get away with lying more times than not. In fact, for some, it is a finely honed skill that has taken years and years of practice.

The key to maintaining the trust of your employees, customers, and shareholders is to *always tell the truth!* The truth is hard to tell when it is bad news: when we have to tell a customer that we cannot ship on time; when we have to tell shareholders that the profit and growth goals will not be met another year; when we have to tell employees that there will be no bonuses this year and that some of them will be laid off. It's really hard to deliver bad news and face the wrath that goes with it.

Organizations that *get it* are those that realize that trust is mostly what they are selling. Give me your money and trust me to invest it wisely. Buy my software and trust me that it will save you money and make life easier. Buy a vacation package from us and I guarantee that it will be a wonderful trip. We're all selling trust, even if we have a product, we're asking customers to believe our advertising. Do you trust your sixteen-year-old? How about your mechanic or dentist? Being caught lying, cheating, or withholding information one time can destroy the trust that has taken years to build up.

So many organizations don't seem to get this simple concept. We forgive most organizations for *mistakes*. We understand that goals are sometimes not met. However, most of us have a hard time forgiving purposeful deceit and lies. A company I work with has a policy that says that honesty is paramount in everything it does.

Employees are taught that anyone caught lying or fudging any numbers will be immediately dismissed without the benefit of disciplinary warnings. The company is known for its honesty and integrity, and works hard to maintain this as part of its culture.

How to Get It: Know What's Important

❏ *Don't create a culture that tolerates lying.* Too many companies and government organizations I've worked with tolerate lying—especially if it is done with good intentions—such as to pacify a customer or keep employees working at full productivity.

❏ *Do look at every interaction as an opportunity to either build or destroy trust.* Trust is hard to earn and easy to lose. Too few organizations understand this—but it's a critical best practice.

GET IT

Learn from Former Customers and Employees

It's bad enough when an organization does not understand what customers and employees want and need to be happy. It's much worse when they leave and you don't find out why. Smart companies probe every lost customer and employee to learn why they left. There are all sorts of excuses why organizations don't gather this data:

- It's too expensive.
- People give you a politically correct answer.
- Customers or employees leave just to try something different.
- It's depressing to look at how we mess up.

An organization that does not *get it* is one that keeps making the same mistakes over and over again and spending millions of dollars to attract new customers and employees, and very little to keep the ones they have. Rarely does a single event cause a customer to take her business elsewhere. Often though, one thing pushes her over the edge and makes the decision.

Lisa had been my travel agent for several years and had usually been great. She always got my tickets to my house, tried to get me upgraded, recorded my mileage and hotel accounts, and got me deals that I would have had trouble getting on my own. Lisa worked at three different travel agencies during the years I was with her, and I went with her each time. But after a few years she started messing things up. At first it was minor and infrequent, and then the mistakes became more serious and more common. She also became hard to get hold of and took a long time to return phone calls and e-mails.

I'm sure Lisa could gauge my frustration, because I always had to call her to get the problems corrected. I never yelled or complained, but she knew I was unhappy. I started using another travel agency on the side for a few trips, and when they proved to do a good job, I stopped using Lisa altogether and never heard from her. If I were Lisa, or her employer, I would want to know why a customer left and what could be done to prevent future customers from leaving. I spend well over $100,000 a year on travel for business and was probably a fairly profitable account for a travel agent.

One of my clients had a similar experience with his employer who does not *get it*. The company was a fun place to work when he started there. It was a small company with many bright people who worked long hours, took many risks, and laughed a lot. Bill eventually got promoted to CFO and the company grew to several hundred million dollars in sales. About five years ago the company was bought by a big corporation, and Bill and the other members of the leadership team who owned stock, did very well. Then things started changing. There were more meetings, more reports and presentations to headquarters, more policies and procedures, less risk taking, no laughing, and, according to Bill, the entire culture seemed to change. He told me a couple of months ago that he retired at age forty-six and no one in the company asked him why he was leaving. He was prepared to give them an earful, but they didn't ask more than the standard three or four exit interview questions.

GET IT

How to Get It: Know What's Important

Former customers, employees, suppliers, or other partners that no longer do business with your organization can provide a wealth of information that can be used to improve your performance. If you take the time to ask and listen, you can find out all the things your organization did wrong that caused the deterioration in the relationship. Here's how to *get it*:

❏ ***Don't let customers or employees just slip away without asking them why they're leaving.*** You'll benefit so much by hearing their answers—and then acting on what they say to change the way your organization does business.

❏ ***Do learn from your mistakes so you don't repeat them.*** Yes, it will be painful and uncomfortable to hear about how you screwed up, and there are always many legitimate reasons for the mistakes. But the bottom line is that if you keep making those mistakes, more and more customers and employees will leave.

Acknowledge Your Weaknesses Rather Than Rationalize Them

Figuring out your strengths is a big part of *getting it*, but just as important is identifying your weaknesses. Organizations spend big money each year to have outsiders conduct audits and assessments. Regulators, consultants, and even internal audit and inspection teams regularly review your practices and performance for the purposes of identifying problems. Those that have been examined for the ISO certification process or applied for a Baldrige type of award learn that this can be a very depressing and sobering experience. The assessors find all the flaws in your organization that you might not have even known about.

As with any audit or assessment, there will be some finds that are off base. Auditors uncover problems that are not really there or make a big deal about little things that you view as perfectly normal. In most of these assessment reports, a number of genuine weaknesses are identified. Often, these things keep coming up over and over again, year after year. When problems are found by regulatory groups, these things pretty much have to be rectified or you will be fined, or possibly shut down. Weaknesses found by your own people, or consultants that you hire, can be dismissed without a problem. Some of them probably should be ignored. There are other things that really need to be fixed and other weaknesses that you will probably never fix.

An organization I worked with for a number of years was very inefficient, and the root causes of most of these inefficiencies was the organizational structure and the processes used to do the work. Accountabilities were shared by many departments so that no one felt ultimately responsible for performance, and processes had many steps that clearly added no value and slowed things down. The organization did have a number of strengths, but doing things quickly and efficiently was not one of them. It eventually learned that it probably would never be a model of efficiency and speed.

Another organization that I worked with was always last-to-market with new technology. It came out with good products that included features that customers really wanted, but it was never first-to-market. One or two of its competitors always seemed to have a new, similar product on the market six months earlier. By the time my client came out with its product, the technology was old news, and the competitors had already sold a lot of their own products. The company eventually figured out that R&D and a quick new product development cycle was not one of its strengths. After years of missing the market window with its new products, it eventually acknowledged that they would probably never beat its two biggest competitors at this game, so its changed its strategy.

Organizations that *get it* are those that realize the things they are not good at or what their inherent weaknesses are. These organizations form their strategies around their strengths and are often quite successful. Perhaps it is a better strategy to let a competitor invest in research and development, only to have its product knocked off by another competitor a few months later. Some companies find that innovation is not one of their strong points, but that stealing and copying are core competencies. There are plenty of successful organizations out there that are not one of the top three in their industry.

G
E
T

I
T

How to Get It: Know What's Important

❏ *Don't ignore your weaknesses, and don't just rationalize them, either.* Don't be stubborn or foolish about what you don't do well, because you'll find it impossible to compete effectively with organizations that are consistently stronger than you in some areas.

❏ *Do acknowledge all of your weaknesses, and then work around those that will probably never turn into strengths.* Focus on your true strengths and find another way to compete.

Learn That Bigger
Is Not Always Better

Can you think of any companies or organizations that were a lot better performers when they were small? How about that restaurant that you and your family went to for years? You knew the owners and they always squeezed you in on a busy Friday night, and they gave you a free dessert every once in a while. Mom and Pop eventually retired, and the two kids, with their college degrees in business, took over and decided to expand into multiple new locations to grow the restaurant business to $5 million in sales. They spent money on advertising, beautiful décor, new menus, staff training, and did their best to copy the ambiance of Mom and Pop's original location. They just couldn't pull it off, and the new locations were viewed in the same light as the local Applebee's, Friday's, or other big chains.

Privately owned companies have more of a choice regarding growth, and they do not necessary need to get bigger. Publicly owned firms generally are expected to grow revenue, and usually that means getting bigger. It is also true that most markets end up being owned by a few giant companies who swallow up the little ones. There used to be over fifty companies that manufactured cars, many of them in the United States and England. Today the car industry is owned by a few giants like Daimler-Chrysler and Ford. No one would even think about getting into the car business today. There used to be a lot of choice when looking for audio equipment as well. Now the market is owned by a few, like Sony, Bose, and Panasonic.

However, many times bigger is not better. Organizations that *get it* understand that there is strength in maintaining small business thinking in a big company. In a small business, you watch every penny, everyone pitches in and does various jobs, and you spend minimal time on administrative things like meetings. Neither small business nor small government has much bureaucracy because there is too much real work to do.

Organizations that *get it* are those that can maintain the small business approach in a big business. Southwest Airlines is one such company. They are known to be very frugal and they minimize the bureaucracy you find in many big corporations. Yet they have grown to be a major player in the competitive airline industry without losing the small-company attitude. Another company that manages this well is Johnson & Johnson. It is made up of many small business units that get very little in the way of corporate interference. This keeps them lean and mean and allows customers and employees to feel like they are dealing with a small company, even though they are part of a huge corporation.

True, there are many advantages to being a bigger company— greater profits, bigger market share, and access to top-notch customers, to name a few. But there are also many risks and downsides to getting bigger. Arthur Andersen grew to be one of the biggest and most successful accounting firms in the world. It had a blue-chip list of clients and hired the best and brightest for its staff. Many of its hundreds of partners earned over $1 million a year. Now that company is pretty much gone. Just because it got too big? No, because as we all know, some of Andersen's key people who were working with Enron broke the law and lied about the Enron company's true financial situation. In contrast, it is easy to control your culture and values in a firm of ten people because you hand select each one and see them each day.

G
E
T

I
T

How to Get It: Know What's Important

❑ *Don't lose sight of qualities like values and ethics, which often happens as a company gets big.* Some people with questionable values sneak past our hiring criteria, or we hire good people who learn that values such as sales are all that matter, and that you need to keep a customer happy—even if that means lying to her.

❑ *Do keep in mind the principles your organization followed in its earliest days, when it was operating either out of a garage or a small storefront.* Size does matter, as we've been told. But the bigger an organization, the more it needs to work on ensuring that everyone stays in touch with customers, the core competencies, and the values on which the company was founded.

Don't Think That You Can't Be Copied

Part of *getting it* is not being too dependent on a product or service that provides a major share of your revenue. Whatever that product or service is will likely be copied and knocked off by someone who will provide it more cheaply. Patents, copyrights, and other devices for protecting the ideas and products that you developed really don't do enough. Fashion designers have their latest designs knocked off and sold by Ross Dress for Less for 10 cents on the dollar six months after they show their new designs at fashion shows. Furniture designers knockoff Henredon and other high-end manufacturers and have copies made in China that sell for a fraction of the real thing. Louis Vuitton comes out with a hot new handbag design that there is year-long waiting list to buy, and some manufacturer in Hong Kong sells exact copies on the Internet. The real thing at LV costs $1200, and the knockoff is $200. Some companies, like Hermes, do a more diligent job of stopping these knockoffs, but they are literally impossible to stop completely. As soon as a knockoff manufacturer is arrested, three new ones crop up.

A handbag or dress is a pretty easy thing to copy and manufacture, but even complex products are knocked off. For years fake Rolex watches have been for sale, and years ago you could always tell they were copies because of the plastic crystals and quartz movements. The fakes have gotten much better now, however, and for about $100 you can buy a Rolex with a sapphire crystal and a self-winding movement with a sweep second hand, just like the real thing. Even the weight is the same as a real Rolex. Sure, you know it is fake, but a lot of other people don't. I took the subway in New York City this summer and was amazed at how many passengers who looked like they hadn't bathed in a while were wearing Cartier or Rolex watches.

The Bentley Azure is a handmade convertible that is one of the fastest, most beautiful, and most expensive cars in the world. At $360,000, it costs more than many people pay for a house. It goes from 0 to 60 mph in less then six seconds, and the driver is swathed in Connelly leather and burled walnut. It truly is a work of art on wheels. Believe it or not, some guy in Miami makes knockoff Bentley Azures that he sells for about $75,000. He starts with the chassis of an Oldsmobile convertible, and builds the Azure body from fiberglass, using many real Bentley parts for the badges and other body parts. He uses Connelly leather for the interior, real burled walnut, puts in a killer sound system, and you can order any color you want. You can even get the car made with a turbo engine that is as fast as the real Azure, or leave the standard GM engine in it. From five feet away you'd swear it was the real thing. Of course, if you slam one of the doors I'm sure you can tell it is cheap fiberglass, but who cares if the valet parking guy at Spago knows your car is a fake—no one else does.

Drug companies typically have a longer shelf life for their prescription drugs before they go generic, or some competitor comes out with a similar product with fewer side effects or at a lower cost. Viagra had the corner on the market for a number of years until recently, when competitors came out with their versions that supposedly work even better. If you have a prescription drug that is a big seller, you can bet that many of your competitors are working diligently to come up with a similar formula to take away your market share.

The only defense against getting ripped off and copied is to always come out with new stuff and stay one step ahead of the knockoff artists. This is easier said than done. Most organizations come out with many new products each year but only a few turn into big sellers. The other companies usually wait to see what sells before they knock you off, so they don't waste money copying a new prod-

G
E
T
I
T

uct that is a dog. Aggressively perusing rip-offs can help, but most are hard to catch and prosecute, or they change your product just enough to avoid a lawsuit. You also have to pay for the attorneys as well as all the R&D that went into the new product in the first place.

Organizations that truly *get it* are those that realize they are going to get ripped off. Someone will copy their products and services if they are successful, so the best defense is to keep coming up with new stuff. An alternative defense is to develop a product or service that is really hard to copy. A rival airline tried to put Southwest out of business ten years ago by starting its own short-distance shuttle. This rival essentially ripped off every part of Southwest's strategy, but there was one thing it couldn't copy—the Southwest culture. So the rival's shuttle no longer exists, and Southwest continues to grow and prosper because it has something magic that other competitors have not been able to copy.

How to Get It: Know What's Important

❏ *Don't become overly dependent on just one product or service (or even just a few).* Eventually, whatever you do really well will be copied and made available for less money.

❏ *Do continue to develop new ideas and products.* The best strategy is to stay ahead of your competition—much better than trying to prosecute imitators—or do something so unique that it simply can't be copied.

Keep Your Promises

Some friends bought a new house recently and in the process of moving had trouble with their phone company. It seems it cut off the phone in the old house five days too soon and were not scheduled to turn on the service in the new home until three days after the new owners had moved in. Not having a phone is not a major crisis for some people, but it is for many. Matt does a lot of his work out of the house and needs to fax in reports to his home office and e-mails, so he couldn't work. His wife was on the phone for several hours with the phone company, most of the time waiting on hold while the minutes continued to add up on her cell phone bill. The whole time she waited on hold to talk to the "next available customer service representative," she listened to a recording about the good service that the company promised its customers.

The promises that companies make to get or keep our business have gotten so common, and are so commonly broken, that we don't pay much attention to them. A few years ago, a major airline came out with a service promise to keep its passengers informed, and to be honest with them. This lasted for about a month; then the airline went back to keeping passengers in the dark and lying to them. Many times I pulled away from the gate on time (because that's how on-time departures are measured), headed out to the runway, and then just sat for forty-five minutes or an hour without anyone saying anything. I was thinking, "What's going on? Why haven't we taken off? Why hasn't the captain said anything?" Meanwhile, I was sitting in the seat looking at the airline's two-page ad in its magazine stating how it promises to keep passengers informed at least every ten minutes.

G
E
T

I
T

Once in a while you find a company that has a promise or guarantee that they live up to. A bank in California promised to pay $5 if you find an error in your bank statement. I can imagine that caused a lot of people to check their statements more thoroughly. A couple of hotel chains have offered the promise of a full refund if you are dissatisfied for any reason, but I think most had to eliminate those guarantees because they were giving away too many free rooms.

A promise or guarantee is a good way of making people feel comfortable about buying your product or service. Organizations that truly *get it* think hard about any promise or guarantee that they come up with *before* launching an ad campaign to announce it to the public. If you make a promise you don't deliver on, it completely destroys your credibility and the level of trust in your organization. It basically tells customers never to believe another one of your ads or claims because you have broken your promise. You promised that you have the widest wireless coverage of any cellular phone company and then the phone cuts out, drops calls, or does not work at all in many cities. You promised to be easy to do business with, and customers can't get through to your call center without waiting on hold for twenty minutes, pressing eight different buttons to get routed to the right place, and then they finally speak with someone who does not understand English well. You promised that the new DSL service would be lightning fast compared to dial-up, but many times screens take several minutes to download or don't load at all.

We are disappointed so often by most big companies that we have gotten to be very wary of any promises that are made. Many people just assume that the promise is a hollow advertising slogan that will never be followed through, or that you are lying and never had any intention of providing the level of performance promised.

Luckily, a few companies do *get it*. The promises they make are real and are kept. The Ritz Carlton follows through on most if its promises and consistently provides guests with exceptional service in all areas of its properties. Of course, for $400 a night, it is a little easier to keep your promises than for $49 a night, but Motel 6 only promises to leave the light on, and it does manage to do that.

Organizations that *get it* keep their promises. They think hard about the kinds of guarantees and promises they can offer to customers, making sure that they link to things customers care about, and then they spend the resources to ensure that the promises can be kept. This is what builds our trust and ensures our future business.

How to Get It: Know What's Important

❏ *Don't make promises about service or product quality that your employees can't keep.* This includes promises to minimize waiting periods for customer service phone inquiries and complaints, to keep customers informed about service problems, and to correct any mistakes the company makes.

❏ *Do keep the promises you make.* Think hard before making any promises, to ensure that you and all your employees can keep them. Make promises that will be appreciated by your customers, and don't stint on the money or time needed to keep those promises. Do whatever it takes, because keeping promises is the core of the trust you're trying to establish with your customers, and it's critical to the success of your business.

Quit Putting Idiots in Leadership Positions

The power of a single CEO seems to be vastly overrated. A great CEO with a weak team will probably still fail. We read books about heroic leaders like Jack Welch, Bill Gates, Steven Jobs, and Herb Kelleher, and think if we could just find someone like that to run our company we would have the leadership we need to be successful. A good leader is vastly important, but so is each member of the management team.

Have you ever had a boss who was a complete idiot? Have you ever met a CEO or high-ranking officer who appeared dead from the neck up? I bet most of you are nodding your heads. In fact, good leaders seem to be relatively rare, and I often wonder how some people got into leadership positions with their major skill deficits and character flaws. In my twenty-five years of consulting, I have met some extremely talented leaders—people whom I wished were my boss back in the days when I had a boss. But in all the great organizations I've worked with, I can only think of a handful of executives that I admired and thought were extremely talented leaders. When I think back, many of them were in the military or government rather than in Fortune 50 corporations. There were a lot more leaders whom I met that made me wonder how they ever got the job they held.

Organizations that *get it* are those that are able to identify management talent and then develop it in their leaders. Rarely do I run into a big government or business organization that does a good job of selecting or developing leaders. Most often, they are selected on the basis of three things:

- The person is strong technically.
- The person is a good soldier and is well liked.
- We need to fill an open position now!

A fourth selection criterion seems to be appearance. Being tall and having good hair and teeth seem to be important for leadership positions. Once in a while, you meet a short, bald leader with bad teeth, but not very often. Appearance is important for women in leadership positions as well, but being too good-looking seems to be a liability for women in top management jobs.

Once someone is on the management track, he or she often continues to get promotions to higher levels of responsibility unless he or she really messes up. The most important thing that organizations with strong leaders do is screen candidates thoroughly for prerequisite talents and traits. How do they do this, and what do they look for? There are certain things a leader needs to walk in the door with. These traits cannot be learned, but are part of a person's genetics and how they were raised. Traits like intelligence, compassion, courage, and honesty cannot be taught and should be selection factors. Many good leadership assessment instruments exist, but too few organizations use them, except possibly on new hires.

Many of us are not well suited to leadership positions. We strive for a leadership job because that is where the money, the power, and the prestige is. Furthermore, leadership is what is expected of us by our peers, parents, and spouses. I've worked with many unhappy engineering managers in big corporations who loved doing engineering work but hated the "people stuff" that they had to deal with as a manager. They weren't very good at the people things, and it was not what they enjoyed, so most of them spent their time micromanaging the engineers' projects and getting involved in details that a manager should not be involved with.

Slotting the right individual in a leadership position is vastly more important than leadership development. No amount of training or coaching can make a good leader out of someone who does not have the prerequisite traits and abilities. Yet organizations often spend many times more money on leadership development than they do on selecting the right people to fill leadership positions.

Part of *getting it* is first realizing that not everyone makes a good boss, and then finding those who will make strong leaders and continuing to hone their skills.

How to Get It: Know What's Important

❏ ***Don't hire or promote people for the wrong reasons.*** Don't appoint people simply out of desperation; don't hire them because they "look" the part of a leader; don't promote people just because they're well liked; and don't try to make great leaders out of people with technical skills but without management and leadership skills.

❏ ***Do keep an eye out for leadership potential and nourish and develop that potential.*** Understand what traits and abilities are most important for leadership in your organization. Then find the right people in the first place, because leadership can't be taught.

GET IT

SET IT

MOVE IT

PROVE IT

Measure What's Important

Once you *get it*, what's next? The next step is to set your direction for the future. *Setting it* is mostly about writing stuff down and keeping track of things. There is not a lot of what most people call "real work" in the *set it* phase. Most organizations don't make any money when they are doing "set it" stuff. *Setting it* is about planning, developing a vision for the future, and identifying performance measures to track your progress and success.

Even an organization as small as mine, Mark Graham Brown & Associates (one guy working out of his house—I don't really have any associates), needs a vision, some goals, and some measures of performance. I don't have a big binder with my strategic plan in it; my vision is simple enough to remember, and I only track a few key performance measures, but all organizations need these basic things to ensure their continued success. Most people would not argue with this logic; it's just that these activities are so often painful, time-consuming, and distracting from the work that makes a company money. You can't really say to a customer, "Sorry, I can't come next week. We have a three-day strategic planning retreat I have to attend."

Planning, setting goals, and developing performance measures do not need to be done at a resort in the woods or a conference center. This work also does not need to be painful, frustrating, and a waste of time. It should be something that you spend a little bit of time doing so that you are more effective doing the work for which you exist, or the things that make you money. This is the stuff I do for a living. I facilitate strategic planning meetings and help design measurement systems or scorecards. Most of the people I encounter tell me they were dreading coming to the meeting or training.

Fortunately, in this part of the book, you will learn that setting goals, developing strategies, and identifying metrics does not need to be painful or a waste of time. You'll learn that there are some common practices that are a waste of time, and hopefully you can stop doing these. You will also learn about some of the best practices I've seen in twenty-five years of consulting with some pretty impressive organizations.

Just about every organization you encounter today has a strategic plan and a set of performance measures they call their balanced scorecard or dashboard. Having these things does nothing to increase your chances of success unless they are done well. Sadly, most are not. Most strategic plans are thick binders of mission and vision statements littered with so many buzz words that Dilbert would be thrilled. Most performance measures look objective and scientific until you dig a little and find that either people have figured out how to cheat on the metrics, or that moving the needle from red to green does nothing to make the organization more successful. Many organizations still have a number of metrics that are tracked once a year, such as an annual morale survey or customer survey. Annual measures of anything are close to being useless because you have to wait twelve months to get another data point and perhaps find out you have major problems.

Believe me, there is a lot of stupid stuff going on in the corporate and government worlds under the banners of planning and measurement. Luckily, doing it right is mostly common sense. Doing it right means:

- Having a clear vision that paints the same picture for everyone who reads it
- Setting goals that are explicit, reasonable, and based on sound intelligence or data
- Creating performance metrics that really tell you how you are meeting the needs of your stakeholders
- Communicating progress without having to sit through a meeting with hundreds of PowerPoint charts
- Using data to measure the success of your strategies and initiatives
- Writing some clear and specific rules that everyone can follow to ensure honesty and integrity

Setting it is about deciding on your future destination and creating a road map to get you there, with mile markers along the route.

Don't Ever Use a Team to Define Your Vision

S
E
T
I
T

Have you ever been to one of those strategic planning retreats where a consultant led the group in creating a vision statement for your company? First you brainstorm all these buzz words that define the kind of company you want to become. After listing thirty to forty of these words, you play around with them in different combinations until you cobble them into a vision statement that everyone likes. After six to eight hours of this frustrating exercise, you end up with something like the following:

Our vision is to become a world-class leading-edge customer-focused supplier of premium goods and services employing an empowered workforce to achieve benchmark level performance in a six-sigma fashion to create real value for our shareholders.

After reading it a few times, you all agree that it sounds great (it's got your buzz word in it) and decide to head for the bar or the golf course. This is not really an exercise in strategic planning; it is an exercise in politics. Everyone wants to make sure the word they suggested appears in the mission statement, and whatever word the CEO suggested always makes it to the beginning of the vision.

Companies seem to believe that you need group consensus on the vision, so it is important to get every team member involved in writing it. Nonsense. I have never ever seen a good vision statement written by a team. Dilbert creator Scott Adams defines a vision statement as "*a long awkward sentence that demonstrates management's inability to think clearly.*"

Getting everyone to buy your vision and support it is important. However, it does not mean that they each need to be involved in writing the sentence. The most successful visions I have seen were created by one person—often the leader or CEO.

A big part of *setting it* is figuring out where you need to be in the future. Visions are usually one of three types: (1) growth, (2) change, or (3) recognition. Once in a while, survival is a legitimate and appropriate vision as well. I worked with a Navy organization that was being examined for possible closure. Its vision was "Still here next year," which was appropriate for its circumstances. A good vision focuses on one thing, not many; it is achievable, in three to five years; and it is inspirational to your employees and other stakeholders. A vision is broader than a goal or a project and should set the organization's course for the future by providing overall direction.

It's easier to create a good vision in a new organization or one embarking on a major change. But what about an organization that has done the same thing for over 150 years? The Norfolk Naval Shipyard has been repairing ships and submarines for well over 150 years and has a clear purpose and mission. Every three years a new Navy captain comes in to take charge of this organization of more than 5,000 people. Each new captain needs to define a vision for his or her three years in charge. The current leader's vision is to "Quit surprising our customers." This is a clear and focused vision, and something that might be achievable in a three-year time frame. Another client has a vision called 50 by 05, which means $50 million in sales by 2005.

Part of the responsibility of being a leader is to define the vision of your organization. It is important to find out what other members of the management team think, but it is ultimately the leader's job to define the vision. I helped the president of a large financial services firm do this by interviewing all his vice presidents and asking them about the direction they thought the company needed to take. I summarized the suggestions of all the VPs, gave the notes to the president, and told him that he had to write the vision, and that he had to write it without using any management buzz words. He actually did a wonderful job, and we spent most of the time in the meeting getting the team of executives to work together to come up with strategies for achieving the vision. You do need a team for that, but you do not need eight people to write a sentence.

S
E
T

I
T

How to Set It: Measure What's Important

❏ *Don't indulge in group consensus to define your organization's mission or vision.* This is one job that should be done by only one person: the top leader. That person can, of course, discuss with others what's most important to the organization, but the final statement needs to be made by one person, so that it will be clear and focused.

❏ *Do determine your mission by deciding where you need to be in the future.* Vision usually involves growth, change, or recognition (by your customers)—although survival occasionally may be the focus. But the most important aspect is that the vision be *specific*—which means being able to prove you have achieved it.

Don't Bother Setting Vague Goals That Will Never Be Achieved

It is important to set goals. Even individuals need to have goals. However, it is discouraging to set goals that will never be achieved. Every year you decide to set a goal to improve your health and lose weight. You sign up for a gym, or buy some walking shoes, healthy food at the grocery store, and maybe even one of those scales that also tells you your body fat percentage. You set some more specific goals and begin the year with the best of intentions, and then you start slacking, you get busy with work, the kids want pizza for dinner, and your parents come for a visit, and before you know it, it is April and you have not made any progress toward your goal.

The same sort of thing happens in organizations when they set goals. Your vision should set the overall direction. The goals provide specifics on the things you want to accomplish. Goals are often narrowed down from a long list made during a planning meeting. I attended a strategic planning meeting of a government client recently, and it narrowed its goals down to three, which is a reasonable number:

- Increase accountability for performance across all employees.
- Improve leadership.
- Increase teamwork and cooperation.

The group felt that these three areas were the biggest problems in the organization, and the next few years should be spent working on these three goals. Teams were formed to address the three goals, and each team met on a weekly basis to develop a detailed plan for achieving the goal.

I sat in on a few meetings of the Accountability Team. After eight weeks of meetings the members could still not agree on what accountability was, how they would know if it improved, and what strategies they could use to improve it. Someone suggested that firing the bottom 5 percent of employees and managers would have a dramatic impact on accountability. Others on the team said that all that would do is increase fear and ruin the good labor relations that had been built over the years. Other suggestions were offered and then shot down, and the group kept disagreeing on what accountability really meant. In the end, it gave up trying to clarify the goal and decided to make a video on accountability and show it to all employees.

Needless to say, the problem was that the goal itself was vague, as were the other two about improving leadership and teamwork. A goal is not the same as a target. A target is a specific number or value on a metric. For example, $2 billion in sales, 5 percent improvement in market share, or 10 percent reduction in defects. Goals specify something you want to accomplish, not the specifics of how you will do it. A goal might be to reduce manufacturing costs, increase customer loyalty, improve employee loyalty, or increase sales in a targeted market.

To test whether or not your goals are clear, ask five people to describe how they will know the goal has been achieved. Ask them what will be different, or what will change if the goal is achieved. If all five give you a similar answer, it is probably a pretty clear goal. If you get five different answers, you'd better rewrite your goals. People like vague goals because it is easier to slide on them. If my goal is "eat healthier," I might feel like I have achieved the goal if I only eat fast food at lunch every day rather than lunch and dinner.

I see a number of companies that actually do set specific goals, but they don't seem reasonable. I remember talking to the head of a Cisco business unit who told me that all Cisco units had a goal of improving sales by 50 percent over the previous year. Fifty percent!

That may have been reasonable during the few years when all the high-tech companies were growing by 50 percent to 100 percent per year, but the tech boom was already waning when Cisco set that goal, and many saw it as unreasonable.

How to Set It: Measure What's Important

❏ *Don't set vague goals.* These are virtually useless, because they're meaningless—literally.

❏ *Do be specific in what you really want to achieve—and be realistic.* When setting your direction for the future, settle on a few (three to five) major goals that are specific and reasonable. They should be improvements or achievements that you actually think you have a good chance of accomplishing, and they should be goals that everyone understands.

**S
E
T
I
T**

Watch Out for "Chicken Efficiency" Measures

When I started my own consulting practice, one of my first clients was a fast-food chain in the fried chicken business. It sent me out to the field to study and document the best practices of its best-performing restaurants. Every restaurant I visited seemed to focus most of its attention on a daily performance metric it had to report: "chicken efficiency." It also had to report sales, but chicken efficiency was viewed as just as important by the managers I spoke with. It turned out that chicken efficiency is a scrap measure of how much cooked chicken had to be thrown away because it sat under the heat lights too long. There were strict standards about how long to leave the chicken under the heat before it got too dried out.

When I asked the top-performing restaurant managers how they achieved 100 percent chicken efficiency each day, they all explained that they stopped cooking and stacking the chicken up under the heat lights two to three hours before the restaurant closed. When customers came in after 6:30, the restaurant would cook to order whatever the customer wanted. Of course, customers had to wait about twenty minutes for the chicken, and many left without buying anything, never to return. When asked about the folly of purposely making customers mad by not having chicken cooked, one manager explained: "The company has no way to measure how many customers come in and leave because we don't have any data on that, but they track chicken efficiency every day."

It's hard to imagine a big corporation encouraging restaurant managers to turn away customers so as not to throw away chicken.

But I've seen chicken efficiency metrics like this in many business and government organizations. Software developers get measured on how many lines of code they write per day, so they write lots of notes in their code so that they look productive. Training managers get measured on how many employees fill classroom seats, even though many sleep through the classes and spend time doing on paperwork they brought to class.

Chicken efficiency measures are those that sound like valid measures but end up driving the wrong behavior. People get pretty crafty when they are being measured on things. Tracking waste or scrap sounds like a valid measure for a restaurant, but if you are not cooking it in the first place to avoid throwing any of it away, that's probably not a good strategy.

The airlines have a great chicken efficiency metric—on-time takeoffs. Sounds like an important measure, but the problem is, they count takeoff when they shut the door of the airplane and the jetway moves back. The planes often sit on the tarmac or runway for forty-five to sixty minutes waiting for a chance to take off. You land late, but the airline reports an on-time takeoff. This is a chicken efficiency measure because it sometimes causes airline personnel to shut the door early, to ensure they look good on this metric. If a passenger walks up ten minutes before departure time, they often won't let her on the plane, even if the jetway is still there. "You need to be here twenty minutes before departure. I'm sorry, but you will have to see if you can get on the next flight." Just like the chicken restaurant, the airlines sometimes turn away customers so they can be sure to shut the door of the plane on time, or early.

S
E
T
I
T

**S
E
T

I
T**

How to Set It: Measure What's Important

The key to having a good set of performance measures is to first think about the behavior you want to drive, or the performance you are looking for, before deciding on the metric. Think about ways in which employees can make the number look good by cheating, or doing things that are not in your organization's best interest. Eliminating these "chicken efficiency" measures will be a major help in developing a set of performance measures that link to your success. Here's how to *set it*:

❏ *Don't measure the wrong things.* If you encourage your employees to keep customer service calls short, and they cut off the customer in order to meet that goal, that's not an effective way to do business—and you'll likely lose customers, who will be frustrated and angry. Similarly, if you encourage your employees to reduce production time, but product quality suffers to meet that goal, that's not effective either.

❏ *Do set realistic goals for what's most important to your organization.* If you want the highest-quality products, recognize that your employees will need sufficient time to achieve that goal—so measure the *quality*, not the time. If your goal is speedy service, make sure you have enough employees and other resources to achieve that goal. Measure what's important to you, because employees will focus on what you're measuring, even if that's not your most important goal.

Writing Stuff Down Does Not Make It Happen

Big organizations love to write stuff down. They have binders filled with policies, procedures, work rules, flowcharts or process models, standards, specifications, appointments, meeting minutes, strategic plans, operational plans, mission and vision statements, team charters, project plans, PowerPoint presentations, and things-to-do lists. Somehow, it makes us feel better to write stuff down.

I recall a training program I attended on time management where we learned to use a cumbersome notebook to write down our personal goals for the week, activities, and so forth. Most of the attendees felt that the approach was too cumbersome and time-consuming, but the company was pushing use of this notebook, so most carried one around and tried to use it. I continued doing consulting work at this company for several years and watched the number of people carrying around bulky planner notebooks diminish each month. One guy I talked to summed it up nicely: "I took the time I used to spend writing stuff down in my planner and now I just do my job instead, so that has added about an hour a day of productive time."

When we write things down it seems like we are doing valuable work: documenting a process, writing a policy, preparing a set of goals. These things all sound like things people at work should be doing. The problem is we spend too much time planning and writing down the things that we're supposed to do, and too little time doing them.

Writing down goals, procedures, or anything does not change anyone's behavior unless they first read it, and then have appropriate resources and consequences for accomplishing what it says they are supposed to do. One of the best business books in recent years is called *Execution*. The authors make some excellent points about the futility of simply writing stuff down. You need to execute—do the job—not just write down what you intend to do.

I remember working with one of the largest aerospace companies that loved to issue new policies to change behavior in the organization. Whenever people were not doing what they were supposed to, corporate issued a new "Corporate Policy Directive" and sent it out to everyone. Some of the policies had been issued many times with multiple drafts, so a complicated coding system soon had to be devised to sort all the policy directives so that CPD 39-a. rev.3 was not confused with CPD 39-a. rev. 2. Do you think that these policies controlled a lot of behavior? Do you think that most people even read them? Of course not. But it made the corporate types feel like they were doing their job.

Remember in the 1990s, when everyone was enamored with process mapping? Using a collaborative team process, we created flowcharts for everything an organization did. We even got ISO 9000 certified based on the excellence of our documentation. The problem is that employees didn't look at the process maps very often so they still did things the way they had always done them, and we even forgot to show them to the new kid who started last week and might have found them helpful.

How to Set It: Measure What's Important

❑ *Don't waste time making unnecessary written documents of what to do, how to do it, and then what you did.* If people spent less time writing stuff down and more time doing their jobs, all organizations could experience an improvement in productivity. Don't get me wrong: documentation is important, and an organization needs procedures, rules, flowcharts, and plans. However, simply writing things down is not enough to achieve performance. We need to execute, not just write about it.

❑ *Do prepare brief to-do lists, policy statements, and procedures manuals—but spend most of your time actually doing the work.* It does help to have a written plan (even a daily to-do list), written goals, and written guidelines to refer to: the best time-management people say that if you write it down, you're more likely to achieve it than if you just think about it abstractly. But it's more important to actually *do* what's on the list. So keep the written stuff brief, so you can get to the job at hand and finish it!

S
E
T

I
T

Beware of the Strategic Planning Retreat

Have you ever been to one of those strategic planning retreats? They are usually held at a resort or conference center, in the woods, which includes a golf course and perhaps a body of water nearby. These two- to three-day events are common practice these days, not only in big corporations but in health care, government, and the military. The typical agenda is to spend half a day listening to presentations about last year's performance. The next half day is spent reviewing the market projections for the coming year, as well as trends in economic, consumer, and regulatory areas that might impact your organization. This first day is basically spent listening to a series of boring PowerPoint presentations of information you have mostly already heard.

The first evening includes some sort of cocktail reception and a dinner at a local restaurant. Everyone jockeys to try to get a seat next to the big boss so they can lobby for their department or program, and earn some extra sucking-up points. The second day often involves a morning activity of goal setting and an afternoon team-building exercise. These team-building exercises are rarely fun; they're often dangerous or embarrassing, and they almost never result in group members getting to like each other more. A more typical result is to learn what jerks some of the people you work with can be.

I attended one such meeting recently where we all had to ride all-terrain vehicles in 40-degree rainy weather. The things were so loud that there was no team building going on because we couldn't talk to each other. In fact, the only interaction that occurred at all was a couple of guys driving fast through mud puddles to splash other guys with sheets of mud. After an hour of being shaken, frozen, soaked, and covered with mud, most of us couldn't wait for this contrived, "fun," team-building activity to be over. Any team building that did occur in the three-day meeting happened in the bar after dinner.

The third day is usually spent listening to each executive lobby for his or her pet strategy to ensure that the effort is given appropriate priority and funding by the group. The end result of the meeting is a bunch of flip charts with some vague goals that come remarkably close to the ones that were set last year and never achieved, perhaps a new draft of a vision statement with a few new Dilbert words thrown in, and some new strategies that were agreed on mostly based on who could argue the most vehemently or had the most convincing sales pitch. Another result is a newfound hatred of some of your team members on the executive team. Overall, the meeting is a resounding failure, and everyone leaves tired and glad to be going back to work the next day.

Don't get me wrong, strategic planning is a huge part of *setting it* and an important part of ensuring that your organization continues to be successful. The problem is that most of these meetings are a waste of time and do not produce a strategy with any substance. Some things to avoid doing in a strategic planning meeting are:

- Listening to presentations about last year's results: Send out this information ahead of time and require attendees to read it.
- Team-building exercises: Have dinner together instead of planning games or activities during the day that take time away from more important things.
- Wordsmithing visions, missions, values, or goals: Arguing about how to word these things with a team of people is frustrating, does not ensure consensus, and is a waste of valuable time.
- Forming teams to work on the goals and strategies for a couple of hours a week: Important goals and strategies need

dedicated resources and are almost never accomplished by a team of people meeting for a few hours a month.

- Agreeing on goals that will not be supported by viable strategies and given appropriate resources to ensure they are achieved.
- Agreeing on goals and strategies for which no measures of success have been identified.

How to Set It: Measure What's Important

Strategic planning is vitally important to your long-term success, but most organizations do it poorly.

❏ *Don't try to develop strategic plans by sending a team to a resort.* Don't waste time on cocktail parties, awards dinners, and so-called team-building exercises that are really just outdoor recreation—not even golf. Those activities have a purpose, but it's not related to serious planning. Don't use the planning process as an excuse for a corporate boondoggle: Strategic planning is too important.

❏ *Do set aside specific time for your top people to focus only on strategic plans.* Plan the agenda carefully and make sure the outcome is a set of measurable goals, strategies, and measures, and that appropriate accountabilities have been defined.

Measure What Matters to Your Success

A big part of setting your future direction is to decide how to measure your progress. Your scorecard, dashboard, or whatever analogy you use to define your performance measures should make your strategy visible to an outside observer. A number of organizations I've worked with track metrics that have questionable value. Some examples of questionable measures I've seen on company scorecards are as follows:

- Training attendance (butts in seats)
- Number of active process improvement projects
- Marksmanship for security officers who never use their guns
- Number of employees with an individual development plan
- Number of processes documented
- Number of active suppliers
- Number of teams

It seems as if organizations like to count things and report on dumb things that are easy to measure but have questionable use for running the organization. I recall working with a state department of transportation in the Midwest that told me that one of the measures it tracked each month was roadkill. Each Department of Transportation truck has a "street pizza identification chart" that they use to identify and record each run-over animal it finds on state roads. Every month the statistics are summarized and the boss comes to the capital to report how many woodchucks, frogs, deer, badgers, or other species of animals lost their lives on state highways. When I asked what they do with the data, or if they ever try to do something to prevent more animals from dying, the response was: "We never do anything with the data; we just report it in meetings."

When you are putting together a gauge, chart, or metric on anything, you need to first think about what you are going to do with the data. Performance measures should all be things that tell you how you are performing for some stakeholder, and should be used to tell you when you need to change your strategies to improve performance. In working with organizations over the years to develop performance metrics, what I have seen is that if something is easy to count, it probably is not that important, unless it is money. The things that are important tend to be hard to measure, and the metrics often involve some judgment rather than simply counting things.

Measuring whether you have the right people with the right mix of skills is critical to most organizations today. Yet, most "intellectual capital" gauges I've seen measure things like training hours per year, education level, or years of experience. All of these things are easy to count, but they don't really measure competence. I've met some Ph.D.s who are dead from the neck up, and other people who never went to college that are brilliant. Years of experience is no guarantee of competence either, since some people have been mentally retired for years, and it seems that those who attend training most often are the employees who don't have enough work to do because no one wants them on a team.

There are many measures that we accept in everyday life that are based on judgment. Baseball is a sport that is mostly based on counting, but there is a little judgment in baseball. Diving is a sport that is measured using a metric that is completely based on judgment. Academy Awards, Baldrige Awards, Emmy Awards, and most other prestigious awards are based on judgment metrics. The secret to a valid judgment-based measure is consistency. Those doing the judging are often rigorously trained, and there are often teams of judges, as in the Olympics or other award programs, to ensure consistency and integrity.

How to Set It: Measure What's Important

❏ *Don't use any metric that is based on counting things other than money.* Too many organizations use metrics that have nothing to do with their core business or with satisfying their customers: they simply count things for the sake of counting things. That's not a good business practice.

❏ *Do make sure that everything you measure somehow gives you information that helps you achieve or maintain your success.* Measure what truly matters to your organization—something that relates to *performance*, that's important to your customers, clients, or other stakeholders.

S
E
T

I
T

Develop
"Cholesterol" Measures

Most of the metrics that companies track are measures of the past. Sales, profits, gross margin, new products introduced, lost time accidents, employee turnover, and market share are all rearview mirror metrics. Don't get me wrong; these outcome measures are certainly important. The problem is that they are all measuring things that have already happened. We can't do anything about a goal we missed last month once last month is over. The customer left, the employee quit, and the money in the budget is gone. Past-focused metrics make up the vast majority of the gauges on many executives' dashboards.

To balance out your scorecard, an organization needs to develop some leading indicators, or "cholesterol" metrics. Cholesterol, weight, blood pressure, and other factors are great leading indicators for your health because they help predict the likelihood of a wide array of health problems like heart attacks and strokes. Most organizations have great heart attack measures and lack blood pressure measures. What this means is that they have to experience a major problem before they realize anything is wrong. By the time they do detect the problem it is often too late. Losing a major customer is a heart attack. So is losing a star executive or leader, or introducing a new product that fails miserably in the marketplace.

Smart organizations don't rely only on these heart attack metrics. Rather, they develop a number of leading indicators that provide them with predictive indicators. Cholesterol measures are not forecasts. Cholesterol measures are real factors that can be tracked and measured with precision. They are often related to factors that you would not care about in and of themselves. If you have high cholesterol you experience no pain or symptoms. You care about cholesterol and blood pressure because these things can be managed and controlled with the right strategy, increasing the likelihood of a long and healthy life.

Some good cholesterol measures I've seen focus on factors such as the strength of relationships with customers, employees, and suppliers. The health of a relationship is a hard thing to quantify, but I've seen some creative indicators developed that look at things like the price of divorce (exit costs), length of relationship, length and strength of contract, referrals, and other variables. Several clients even include political connections in rating the strength of a relationship with customers. For example, if your CEO plays tennis on a regular basis with the customer CEO, and they are friends, this helps ensure that the relationship between the two organizations continues.

Another client has developed some good measures of the amount of creativity and innovation going on in the company. Metrics include things like suggestions from employees, industry firsts, awards, patents, and even failed business ventures and ideas. The company believes that if it does not have many failures each year it is not taking enough risks and being innovative. Many successful products are the result of many failed prototypes. The guy who invented the Dyson vacuum made over 4,000 prototypes before he hit on one that worked better than any vacuum cleaner on the market. Taking risks and failing is a characteristic that may be a cholesterol metric that links to an outcome like new product sales.

**S
E
T
I
T**

How to Set It: Measure What's Important

❏ *Don't only look at the past when measuring performance.* Although it's important to know how your organization did last year, for example, in terms of sales, profits,
market share, customer satisfaction, and the number of
new products introduced, it's also important to have some
predictive, leading indicators of how you're doing.

❏ *Do try to make at least one-third of your metrics be
leading indicators, or "cholesterol" measures, when
you are putting together your scorecard of gauges to
monitor company performance.* I call them cholesterol
measures because they predict the likelihood of problems
arising, preventing you from simply waiting for the big
"heart attack" that can debilitate your company. Initially,
you will have to do some research to test the validity of
your leading indicators. But once you have the data to
prove the correlation between your leading and lagging
indicators, you can concentrate on managing those variables that help you *predict* success rather than sit in
monthly meetings and get depressed looking at things that
have already happened.

Focus on Doing Your Mission Well Before Chasing a Vision

Setting goals for the future should mostly focus on your mission or job, rather than on your vision. This is kind of like making sure that you have oil, gas, and water in the car before worrying about how to win the race. Without taking care of the basics, you're not even in the race. When you develop a strategic plan, it should include goals that relate to the core business or mission, and a few strategic goals that link back to the vision. Setting goals that relate to the core business is boring and mundane. Strategic goals and measures are sexy, exciting, and require some innovative thought. Consequently, the basics are often forgotten while an organization is off chasing its vision.

A good rule to follow is that 80 percent of your measures and goals should link to your mission or core business. The remaining 20 percent should be more strategic in focus and link to your vision.

Mission-related goals and measures should focus on core things like sales, margins, new products, employee morale, intellectual capital, safety, productivity, quality, cost control, and hitting project milestones. Every year you need to set goals in all these areas. Some real thought needs to be put into these basic goals. You need to look at what is going on in the world economy, your market, technology, regulations, politics, and other factors that might affect your organization. This situation review is usually done as part of most planning meetings, but once these slides are finished they are quickly forgotten, and goals and strategies are often developed without any thought of what is going on in the world. "I don't care about the recession, we're still going to set a goal of a 15 percent increase in sales over last year."

One of the keys to setting goals well is to run each goal by the screen of situational factors you outlined to see if it still makes sense. Summarize the situational factors by category such as:

- Economic
- Political
- Regulatory
- Technological

Review each proposed goal against the facts in each of these situational categories and ask the group attending the planning meeting to explain how the goal can be achieved given the facts of your situation. Of course, it is always possible to rationalize the goals by challenging the validity of the situational findings. This is typically what happens and what leads to strategic plans becoming out of touch with reality. The facts defining your current and future situation should be well researched to minimize the challenging and rationalizing.

After reviewing the goals against the facts of your situation and making necessary changes, the next step is to review them against each other. There are often contradictions here that will make achievement of all of the goals next to impossible. For example, one might ask how it would be possible to reduce costs, increase sales, and improve morale. Improving one aspect of performance often requires the price to be paid elsewhere, Remember when everyone had a TQM program and a stringent goal of reducing defects to near six-sigma performance? Quality got better because of the focus, but often at the expense of morale, profits, or other factors. Think about the interrelationships between the various goals and measures to make sure that you are not setting impossible goals. Keep in mind that raising the bar each year on everything is a good way to drive yourself nuts.

How to Set It: Measure What's Important

Setting goals linked to your mission and vision is an important activity for any organization. It is rarely done well, however. The keys to success are to make sure that most of the goals relate to your core business and that both strategic and operational goals are realistic and achievable. Here's how to *set it*:

❑ *Don't get overly caught up in the excitement of strategic planning at the expense of working to fulfill your organization's basic mission.* Strategic planning is often perceived as "sexier," but only 20 percent of your planning time should really be devoted to chasing a vision.

❑ *Do spend 80 percent of your planning time on goals that link to your core business.* These goals should pertain to such critical business factors as sales, profits, productivity, quality, costs, and morale, to name just a few. First pay attention to the basics, the essence of your business, and make sure these goals make sense and are achievable.

**S
E
T

I
T**

Spell Out Right and Wrong

Setting it is about setting goals, defining your future vision, and developing performance measures. It is also about setting rules about how employees and others behave. Every week we read about another company that has been caught doing something corrupt or, at the very least, unethical. In Part I, I talked about the importance of defining a set of clear and realistic values that should serve to define your culture, Values are not enough on their own, however, because even the best ones leave a lot of room for interpretation. What's needed is a set of rules.

Remember when you were in grade school? There were a lot of rules back then. There were rules about raising your hand to ask a question, talking in class, chewing gum, interrupting others, pushing, and cheating. It did not take long to learn these rules, and the few kids who did violate them usually experienced immediate negative consequences. As kids go from elementary school to middle school to high school, the rules become fewer, and more of our behavior is left to our own judgment. By the time we get to college, there are very few rules. If we want to get drunk and stay out all night, be rude to other people, and sleep through class, it is pretty much up to us. We still experience the consequences of our actions, and that serves to keep most of us in line.

So, part of college is about growing up and learning to control your own behavior so that you can be successful and liked by others. Then you get a job, and there are some rules, but work rules are usually pretty vague and leave much to individual judgment. A lack of clear and specific rules about your behavior and a lack of consequences is what has led to ethics crises in many large organizations.

It always starts with little things. Someone takes a friend out to dinner and charges it to her company credit card, saying it was a client. Someone else puts $20 on his expense report for a cab ride that never happened. The CEO asks public relations to "spin" a news release to make results look more positive than they really are. A salesperson makes a promise to a customer that she knows can never be fulfilled. People learn to look the other way at these small and insignificant indiscretions. Over time, the unethical behavior becomes more common and more serious. People I talk to rationalize their actions by complaining about the pressure they are under and the long hours they are putting in, so they feel it is okay to cheat a little. Left unchecked, your organization may find itself in the situation of WorldCom or Enron.

A big part of the solution is to have clear and explicit rules governing employee behavior. There is very little unethical behavior in most military and federal organizations I've worked with, because the rules are clear, and the consequences for violation are severe and immediate. The rules are sometimes a little silly, like I can't buy my Navy client a sandwich at lunch even if she buys me one the next day, but the rules are consistently followed by everyone I've encountered. Business can learn a lesson from government on rules. Rules need to be so clear that there are few gray areas left to individual judgment. Faulty judgment is how a lot of big companies have gotten into trouble.

S E T I T

S
E
T

I
T

How to Set It: Measure What's Important

Setting it is more than goals and measures. Rules need to be set that give employees and other stakeholders clear guidance on right and wrong. Here's how to *set it*:

❏ ***Don't leave ethics up to the individual judgment of employees: This is very dangerous.*** Furthermore, simply setting the rules and communicating them is not enough, either. If that were the case, we would not need police officers, judges, and jails. Organizations also need to have a system for ensuring that the rules are enforced. What this typically means is a lack of tolerance for even small rule violations.

❏ ***Do establish clear rules of behavior for all employees to follow.*** This will help your organization avoid breaches of ethics in all areas of business—including customer service, public relations and publicity, sales and marketing claims, and, of course, accounting.

Planning Is Not About Creating a Binder or Brochure

Federal government organizations are heavily into strategic planning these days. Much of this activity began years ago with the Government Performance and Results Act, which said: Thou shalt have metrics and a strategic plan. Government organizations began the same struggle that corporations began years earlier in creating mission and vision statements, and writing goals and measures. To their credit, some of the government strategic plans I've seen are very creatively prepared. In fact, I have one in my desk drawer from the U.S. Department of Education (DOE) that looks like a tiny lesson book. It is only two inches by three inches and includes only six major goals, with each having between two and six subgoals. The format is convenient, innovative, easy to read, and I bet most DOE folks keep a copy in their planning notebooks or desks. As a method of documenting and communicating the strategic plan, this is one of the most creative I've seen. Of course, some of the goals are quite vague ("Create a culture of achievement," or " Establish management excellence"), but the format is very cool.

Corporations don't like to publish their plans as brochures or pamphlets; they tend to favor big binders. Of course, even government organizations tend to have the real strategic plan in a big binder that only senior leaders get a copy of. A major outcome of many planning organizations is writing this big planning binder and keeping it up to date as measures, targets, goals, and strategies change. Keeping these documents up to date is a massive job, and there is a big problem with the binders and brochures I've seen: They don't contain any real goals or strategies. The focus seems to be on creating the binder or brochure, rather than on selecting a strategy for winning the race. Planning is not about creating a binder or brochure. Planning is about figuring out:

- How to keep a competitor from stealing your customers and employees
- How to prove your value to taxpayers and Congress
- How to go from being a little player to becoming a big player with major market share
- How to differentiate your company from the many others that sell the same stuff
- How to develop a strategy that not only works, but that competitors can't steal

In short, planning is not a writing exercise, it is a thinking exercise. The reason why so many plans are so vague and lack substance is that there is a "group think" approach of getting everyone to reach consensus on everything. In the spirit of teamwork and consensus, important goals and strategies are watered down and modified so as not to offend anyone, so all you are left with are plans that don't really say anything. In order to get everyone to agree on things, we change the words so that no one can really hold us accountable for not achieving our goals.

I remember one federal government facility I worked with that wrote a really clear goal: "Get more work." This goal was clear, measurable, and could be easily recalled. After the strategic planning team finished with it, it became a long awkward sentence that talked about "outreach" (marketing is a dirty word in government) and taxpayer value to maximize the resources of—blah, blah, blah. By the time the group reached consensus on the goal, no one knew what the hell it said.

To ensure that your plans have real substance, focus more on the strategizing and thinking part of the process than on the documentation part. One shipping company I worked with never bothered to write a strategic plan. Rather, it figured out three key ways that it could differentiate itself from other shipping companies. It taught every employee how they could contribute to these strategies, and it achieved every one of its goals without a binder or brochure. What it did have was a strategy.

How to Set It: Measure What's Important

❏ *Don't focus your valuable planning time on writing the "big planning binder" of targets, goals, strategies, and measures you're tracking.* These binders just suck up time: time to create them and time to maintain them as plans change and are updated. Moreover, they don't seem to include the organization's specific goals and strategies.

❏ *Do approach planning as a thinking exercise, rather than a writing exercise.* The best strategic plans are simple, to the point, and brief. Your planning time should focus on how your organization is going to differentiate itself from others, how to compete effectively, how to increase its customer base, and other critical business goals. Focus your time and efforts; don't waste it on just writing stuff down.

S
E
T

I
T

Measure the "How" as Well as the Outcomes

S
E
T
I
T

Process is a big word these days. We have process maps, process documentation, process control, and process improvement teams. What I don't often see is good process measures on the scorecards of most organizations, At the executive level, most measures should focus on outcomes like profits, happy employees, and returning customers. Once you drill down into the second or third tier of metrics, there needs to be some process measures that link to the outcome measures. An approach I've often seen for creating this linkage is called strategy mapping. The basic idea is to start with an outcome like profit and work down several layers to subsidiary measures. For example, profit might drill down to sales and expenses. Expenses might drill down to direct and indirect; direct might drill down to labor and materials; labor expense might drill down to salaries and benefits, and so forth. This one's pretty obvious, and the relationships are well known.

A lot of organizations make a mistake in creating these drill-down strategy maps when they fail to define process measures and standards that have been proven to link to outcome measures. A call center I worked with had a process metric called "speed to answer," which was a measure of how long the caller waited on hold to talk to the "next available customer service rep." Because it focused on this process measure, good performance was generally achieved. Call center employees learned that they could keep this measure looking good by getting customers off the phone quickly and getting on to the next call. There was no measure that looked at answering the customers' questions or solving their problems, only how long they waited on hold. Hence, there was no real link between the process measure of hold time and customer satisfaction, repeat business, or any other meaningful outcome.

It is important to have process measures that drive outcome measures. Most of the good ones I've seen come from manufacturing organizations. Manufacturing organizations such as paper mills or steel mills monitor and control process variables such as speed, pressure, temperature, and other factors that link to good quality steel or paper. Process variables are determined through experimentation, so the process metrics are valid and do link to outcomes.

In government and service organizations, process measures are based on politics, superstition, theories, or what is easy to measure. A state health and welfare organization had a goal of improving the health of its state residents, as measured by factors such as mortality, and some leading indicators such as blood pressure, weight, and drug or alcohol use. The problem was they did not really have any hard data on how unhealthy or healthy the state residents were, so it decided to measure program or process variables. It measured such things as how many residents attended state-sponsored weight loss and quit smoking clinics, got their kids immunized, attended exercise classes, participated in rehab programs, and other factors. Essentially, it measured attendance in state-sponsored programs. According to its process measures, it was exceeding its goals. During that same time, one of the biggest cities in the state was listed as one of the unhealthiest cities in America by a major magazine. The magazine looked at outcome measures such as cigarette sales, fast-food sales, and early deaths from car accidents, heart attacks, and strokes.

SET IT

**S
E
T

I
T**

How to Set It: Measure What's Important

❏ *Don't set your process measures by superstition instead of by research.* Service organizations need to learn an important lesson from their manufacturing cousins. Part of having a balanced set of measures is to make sure you have some process measures on most scorecards. The test of whether you have picked the right ones is to see if improvement in the process measure causes a related improvement in one or more outcomes enough times to convince you that your hypothesis was right. Measuring outcomes alone dooms you to failure, because it is often too late before you realize the problem. However, superstitious or poorly defined process metrics give you a false sense of security that everything is okay, when maybe you should be worried.

❏ *Do drill down from the outcomes you're targeting and find out what processes you need to measure to achieve those outcomes.* For example, if your goal is to increase profits, you need to measure that process—i.e., increasing sales and reducing expenses.

Focus on Only a Couple of New Things Per Year

Successful organizations never overplan or underexecute. However, this is a common practice in many large organizations. Each year they set some aggressive goals for themselves and identify some important strategies that will lead them toward their vision. The next year, they get together and sheepishly admit that most of the goals have not been achieved. I worked with a major aerospace company for seven years and each year helped its business units assess their strengths and weaknesses. Management mostly agreed with our findings and wrote "closure plans" wherein it identified goals, measures, and strategies for fixing the weaknesses identified. The following year the audits revealed many of the same faults plus some new ones that had cropped up. We did this for many years until the organization finally decided to stop doing the assessments and improvement plans.

Another big corporation I worked with for many years had a different approach. Minneapolis-based Cargill is the largest privately owned company in the world and one of the best companies I have ever had the privilege of working with. Like the aerospace company, Cargill assessed each one of its business units every year against the Baldrige Award criteria. Senior management reviewed the summaries of strengths and weaknesses of the various business units, looking for common themes. Each year it picked one major initiative or area of weakness in the company to fix. One year it was metrics. Most businesses had only financial measures and almost all of them were rearview mirror or past-focused metrics. For an entire year, the company focused on building balanced scorecards for its business units. This was the only big improvement initiative for the year because the company realized that its businesses were busy doing their jobs.

During seven years of working with this company, I watched it improve each year because each year it picked only one major weakness to fix, and it actually improved in the areas targeted. It went from the very beginnings of the Baldrige scoring scale to winning the award in one of its business units.

The aerospace company never even applied for the Baldrige Award, even though one of the CEO's long-term goals was to win it. Both of these two big corporations are filled with smart hardworking people and both had executive support for the improvement activity. My view of the reason for success of one and failure of the other is that the second company was very careful not to try to fix too many things at once. All companies have a long list of weaknesses to go with their strengths. You can go broke very quickly trying to fix everything. An assessment against the Baldrige or ISO criteria can be a depressing and eye-opening exercise—learning all the things you do wrong or don't do. There is a natural tendency to try to fix all the things the auditors find wrong with your company. Resist this temptation!

How to Set It: Measure What's Important

❑ **Don't try to improve everything that's wrong with your organization at the same time.** It's simply not possible, and you'll most likely end up improving nothing at all.

❑ **Do focus your attention on improving one specific weakness at a time.** Smart organizations realize that they have limited time and limited resources, and that they need to be very selective when it comes to setting improvement goals and deciding on weaknesses to fix. Follow the approach taken by Cargill and pick one or two improvement initiatives per year, rather than a dozen or more. The key to setting your future goals is to realize that there is much work to do in performing your basic mission or job, and that leaves only a few hours a week to be spent on improving things for the long term.

Customer Surveys Are Usually a Waste of Time

Customer surveys are cheap, easy, and done by just about every organization in the public or private sector that is even a little concerned about customer satisfaction. They used to be popular with only a few industries, such as hotels and car companies, but now it seems like everyone is conducting these surveys. You get surveys from your gardener, kids' teachers, dentist, travel agent, Internet service provider, bank, credit card company, mechanic, and just about anyone else that you buy something from or pay to perform some service for you. Not only are you inundated with these customer surveys at home, you get them at work too. Human Resources wants to know how it is doing; so does Information Technology, and Procurement.

I don't know about you, but I fill out less than 10 percent of the surveys I receive. I find that two types of people tend to fill out customer surveys—those who really hate you and are mad, and those who are bored or lonely or don't have enough work to do. Most of the rest of us just don't have time—particularly if things are okay. Telephone surveys are slightly better than mail surveys because you get more people to respond, but you also make more people mad by calling and asking them to participate in a survey. Lonely people seem to really like the telephone surveys because they are glad for the chance to have someone to talk to. The rest of us just don't want to be bothered by these pests.

Customer satisfaction surveys are notoriously unreliable as predictors of future buying behavior. I've worked with a number of organizations that have watched many "very satisfied" customers leave and start doing business with a competitor. Some car companies have shown dramatic improvements in customer satisfaction scores, yet owner loyalty remains around 40 percent. Customers may really be satisfied but get lured away by a competitor with a sexy new product or cheaper price. Another problem with surveys is that the ratings you receive are based on the most recent experience with your organization and may not reflect your overall performance. A shipping company found that customers forgot the twenty other packages that were delivered on time throughout the year. If the last package sent before the survey went out was late, the company got bad marks from customers.

Everyone tells us that we need to measure how well we satisfy our customers, but how do you do this without asking them by using some sort of survey? Remember in Chapter 6, I talked about figuring out what aggravates customers? Well, I have had several clients use a good measure called a customer aggravation, or surprise, index. They track, on a daily basis, how much they aggravate their customers because of poor service (e.g., waiting on hold or in lines) or poor quality (mistakes, claims, defects, etc.). Mistakes and screwups are usually coded based on their severity, so a minor mistake is not counted the same as a major flub. For example, a minor problem might be waiting on hold for fifteen minutes to make an airline reservation by phone. A major aggravation might be a cancelled flight because of mechanical problems in a city where every hotel is booked, so customers have to spend the night in the airport.

Tracking things like broken promises, screwups, mistakes, or simply aggravations is usually much better than a survey. Most will forgive an organization's mistakes a few times, but eventually we reach a boiling point and simply take our business elsewhere, never to return. Even a number of government and military organizations I've worked with have developed a measure like the customer aggravation, or surprise, index. In their cases, customers often have no choice, but to do business with them. Nevertheless, they still want to measure how well they take care of their customers without aggravating them too much or screwing up too much.

How to Set It: Measure What's Important

If you are conducting a customer survey, keep doing it if you think you get a good return rate and that the data is helpful. If you are not doing one, don't start. Find better ways to measure how well you meet customer needs without bothering them with yet another survey. Here's how to *set it*:

❏ ***Don't rely on customer surveys to find out what customers think of your organization.*** Few people fill them out, and many of those who do are motivated by their most recent experiences which will skew your data results. Most people just don't have the time, or don't want to spend it filling out the numerous surveys they receive from myriad sources.

❏ ***Do keep track, daily, of what truly aggravates your customers.*** Also, make sure these are important problems, not just trivial or petty annoyances. Then you'll know where your true weaknesses are and you can focus on improving and fixing them.

**S
E
T

I
T**

Set Targets Scientifically, Not Arbitrarily

S E T   I T

A metric without a target is pretty useless. Imagine getting your blood pressure tested and having no idea whet the numbers mean. The information would not really help you until the doctor explained the healthy and unhealthy ranges for the two numbers that make up your blood pressure metric. The same thing holds true with business measures. A good metric becomes meaningless without an equally good target. Targets define the level of acceptable or desired performance, for example, $2.5 billion in sales, less than 12 percent employee turnover, or a 40 percent gross margin. The metric is sales or turnover, and the $2.5 billion or 40 percent are the targets. A number of organizations I work with develop three layers of targets:

- Red—we're in big trouble and performance is bad.
- Yellow—we should watch this metric closely because performance is okay but not great.
- Green—we are achieving desired performance.

One client uses purple to indicate performance that exceeds the targets. Most scorecard software allows you to use whatever colors you want.

Sometimes targets are set as ranges, as with process measures; at other times they are absolute values. Sometimes it is not important to achieve a specific number; anything in a range is OK. Many health metrics like heart rate, blood pressure, and cholesterol indicate good performance as ranges. These ranges are sometimes adjusted when new data indicates this is necessary.

I am amazed at the number of huge corporations and government organizations that pull their targets out of thin air. You can always spot these arbitrary targets because they are round numbers: 90 percent customer satisfaction, 10 percent cost reduction, 20 percent reduction in defects, and so forth. When I ask how these targets were derived, the typical answer is either:

- "We looked at how we did last year and bumped it up a bit," or
- "We just guessed what we think it should be because we have no baseline data."

There are big problems with setting your targets arbitrarily. One problem can be that you are looking at performance and assume everything is fine because you are hitting your target when, in fact, you should be very worried. You might be hitting your arbitrary target and performing much worse than a competitor who could steal your customers. An equally serious problem with arbitrary targets is that you spend valuable resources like people and money to move performance much higher than it really needs to be. Many companies learned this lesson when doing total quality management programs years ago. They improved quality to the point that it cost them their profits.

So, if you don't set targets arbitrarily, how should they be set? Targets should be set based on the following information:

- Your past performance over multiple years
- Competitor performance
- Industry averages
- Customer and stakeholder requirements
- Situational factors like the economy and politics
- Resource constraints:
  - Technology
  - Facilities
  - Budgets
  - Headcount

All these factors need to be sifted through to arrive at what looks like a reasonable and achievable target.

S E T I T

How to Set It: Measure What's Important

❏ *Don't set arbitrary stretch targets.* This is usually a waste of time, and it does more to discourage good performance than drive performance to new heights.

❏ *Do make sure that every target is based on research, not pulling numbers out of the air.* This will help your organization ensure that your gauges really tell you what you need to know.

Think About What It Will Take to Achieve Your Goals

My friend Joe and his partner have worked hard over the years to build up their two-person consulting and training firm to forty employees, with a number of big-name clients and multimillion-dollar contracts. Joe and his partner are raking in the dough and have achieved their goal of creating a successful firm with blue chip clients. Joe wrote a book that was on the *Los Angeles Times* best-seller list and manages to spend several weeks a year at his house in Hawaii, where he hopes to retire some day. Joe is the envy of a lot of people for what he and his partner have been able to accomplish, but it has not been without big costs.

I had dinner with Joe the other night and he told me he is on the road at least four days a week now, and works six days a week. He gets seventy-five to one hundred e-mails per day from clients and employees that he responds to after working all day; he often gets over twenty phone calls per day and always has to keep his cell phone on. He has not had time to surf in years or do a lot of things he used to do—the business is just too demanding. His company has meetings at 7:00 on Saturday mornings because that is the only time everyone is in town. Yes, he is appreciative of his success. He has a wonderful marriage, great kids, a house by the beach in California, and another in Hawaii. But Joe says he thinks he was happier when he made less money and his life was much less complicated and demanding.

Big organizations often run into the same dilemma as Joe and his small company. We set all these goals to become a big successful force in the marketplace, and through hard work and a little luck, we achieve our business goals. Rather than enjoying our success, we miss the old days when the company was a fun place to work and everyone was not quite so overworked. A part of planning, often forgotten, is to think hard about each goal to make sure it is what you really want. More important, you need to think about what it will cost to achieve the goal and if it is worth it.

When developing your goals, plans, and strategies, each one needs to be challenged before you agree to it. We don't spend enough time really thinking hard about each goal and what it will mean if it is achieved. With every move forward or change, something is often lost. For every goal that is achieved, there are bad things that go with the goal. You get that big account you have been working on for two years, and the client is the biggest pain in the butt you have ever experienced. You move into the new high-rise that took three years to design and build, and employees hate it because they see each other only on elevators now, and parking downtown is a nightmare. You finally achieve your vision of number one in market share and find that your competitors are constantly poaching your star employees.

In short, there is a price to pay for every goal that is achieved. The downside, risks, or costs to achieve goals is not a popular thing to bring up in planning meetings. Those that do are often labeled as cynical, jaded, or whiners. So, everyone stays upbeat and positive, and thinks about how much better the organization will be if the vision and goals are achieved. Two approaches should be part of every planning meeting. First of all, make sure that goals are set for all aspects of performance, not just financial. Balancing your goals so that there are an equal number that relate to customers, shareholders, and employees will help assure that there is not too much focus on one type of stakeholder.

The second approach that I've seen work well is to do a risk and cost-benefit analysis on each goal. In other words, think about what could go wrong in your quest to achieve each goal and the likelihood of any of these things happening (risk analysis). Then, identify all of the costs required to achieve the goal (including intangibles like change in the business culture) and weight them against the benefits. The benefits should be expressed in dollars, but in other measures as well. For example, a benefit of landing a big name client might be a boost in your brand image and credibility with other potential customers. If all of the goals pass the balance test, the risk test, and the cost-benefit test, then proceed to put out the strategies and resources to make them happen.

How to Set It: Measure What's Important

❏ *Don't ignore the price of success.* Every goal you achieve will change your organization in some way, so you need to be prepared for that. If you increase your customer base, you need more time (and probably staff) to serve those customers. Don't forget to make allowances and plan for these ramifications when you're setting goals and strategies. In other words, be careful what you wish for because you might get it.

❏ *Do think about what the result will be on all aspects of your business if you achieve the goals you set.* Also, be sure to balance your goals so that you don't focus too much on any one stakeholder. Finally, do a risk analysis and a cost-benefit analysis for every goal you're targeting.

**S
E
T

I
T**

Align Goals and Plans— Find Disconnects

S
E
T

I
T

My friend Jim left this morning for St. Louis for his company's annual planning meeting. Jim manages the West Coast sales region and had prepared his goals prior to the meeting. He was not given any overall company goals, so he had to take his best guess about how to set his own targets. Last year the same thing happened, with each unit of the company bringing its goals to the meeting. Most people just took their actual performance from the previous year and bumped it up by 5 to 10 percent to conform with the company's typical sales goal of a 10 percent increase from the previous year. Some managers were more aggressive with their goals, and some wrote goals that were a real stretch. When questioned about the strategies for achieving the goals, the managers often had created some unusual and creative strategies.

The problem with all this independent goal setting and strategy development is that the company's efforts were poorly aligned. This led to wasting resources, one unit suboptimizing the results of others, and a lack of focus in company strategy. Poorly aligned goals and plans is probably one of the more common problems I see in medium and large organizations. One financial services client I worked with had a step in its planning process that we called "Find the Disconnects." Draft copies of the goals and plans were distributed to a team responsible for overall company planning, and the team worked to find the inconsistencies and disconnects in the various plans. Some things that the teams found were fairly minor, like targets or goals that did not correspond well to one another, or strategies that were slightly different. Some of the bigger problems had to do with strategies and goals that were completely incongruent with the company direction. For example, the risk management unit had goals and strategies that involved tighter credit standards and screening to reduce losses. The marketing group's goals centered around growth by bringing in new customers, which involved more lenient credit standards and risk.

The Find the Disconnects activity turned out to be so critical that the following year a large group was used to do the analysis. The group was divided into teams, and teams were given points for the number and types of disconnects they found. This approach not only allowed the company to identify a number of inconsistencies in its plans, the points and competition between the teams made the analysis fun. Prizes were given to teams that earned the most points in the game.

A better approach than reworking your goals and plans after inconsistencies are found is to do it right from the start. Smart organizations begin by writing the goals and plans for the entire company first. After the overall plans are reviewed and approved, the executives at the next level develop their goals. Responsibilities for supporting and achieving company goals are assigned up front. For example, each of the five sales regions might own 20 percent of the overall sales goal, while support departments like Finance and Human Resources have no ownership of the sales goal. Finance and some of the line departments might own parts of a goal related to cost reduction, however. The point of this top-down approach is to ensure alignment and accountability for achieving company goals.

Planning a layer at a time, starting from the top, is the most logical approach for ensuring consistency and ownership. The major drawback is that the planning process takes a long time to complete. A number of big corporations I've worked with take four to six months each year to complete the plans, because each layer has to wait for the next level up to complete its plans. By the time you get down to departmental plans, you could be six months into the year and only have half of the year left to achieve your goals.

Planning is a process that should require four to six weeks per year to complete; not four to six months. It should be done from the top down, but it should also be done in a few weeks. To achieve this four- to six-week window and still create the plans in a top-down fashion requires a concentrated effort, and very quick documentation and communication of higher-level plans to the next level.

S E T   I T

How to Set It: Measure What's Important

❑ *Don't ask employees to set their own goals until you've set the organization's overall goals.* When employees set their own goals first, there are often "disconnects" and inconsistencies, where one person's or department's goal directly contradicts another's. Obviously, that's not effective. If you've already done this, at least have someone review all the individual goals to make sure they don't compete with each other.

❑ *Do write the plans and goals of the entire organization first, then drill down layer by layer from the top.* Instead of reviewing individual goals after the fact, prevent the problem from occurring in the first place. Start with the overall strategy and specific goals; then have each department declare how it will work to achieve subsets of those goals; then have each (relevant) individual declare how he or she will work to meet the department's goals. But don't take forever to do this: make sure the drill-down planning process keeps moving—and moves swiftly.

GET IT

SET IT

MOVE IT

PROVE IT

Do What's Important

Small organizations spend almost all of their time *moving it*, and are often too busy to do things like strategic planning and market research. All phases of the model are important, and even small organizations need to spend some time figuring things out and planning. *Moving it* means doing the work that makes you money or relates to your mission. *Moving it* is cooking the food, flying the plane, manufacturing the product, fixing the car, teaching the kids, or whatever you do for a living. A well-run organization should spend 70 to 80 percent of its efforts doing its mission, and the remaining 20 to 30 percent *getting it*, *setting it*, and *proving it*. The bigger and more complex the organization is, the least amount of time it seems to spend getting its basic work done. Universities and schools often devote less than 50 percent of their budgets and resources to education. The same is often true of hospitals in terms of the extent to which their resources are devoted to patient care.

To recap, *getting it* is figuring out what customers want, what you are going to do, and what you believe in. *Setting it* means establishing a vision, some goals, plans and strategies. *Moving it* means execution, getting the job done—doing the work rather than thinking about it or planning it. *Moving it* also includes moving the needles on the performance gauges you created in the *set it* phase.

Nonperforming people and organizations love the *get it* and *set it* phases of the model, because this type of work is usually easier and demands less effort than actually performing mission-related tasks. There is so much paper pushing and meeting going on that some big organizations seem to forget why they exist.

In this part of the model, there are two keys to good performance. One has to do with people, the other with process. A critical factor for any organization is having the right team of people with the right mix of skills, knowledge, and values. Many organizations I encounter spend far too little time selecting the right people and far too much time trying to train and develop people who don't have the capabilities they need in the first place. Another misconception about the *move it* phase of the model is that activity or behavior equals results. Sadly, this is rarely the case.

I observe far too much unproductive behavior in organizations. Everyone is busy, working long hours, responding to twenty phone calls a day, reading seventy-five e-mails a day, and going to endless meetings. Yet much of this activity does not make any of the important gauges on the corporate dashboard move. Sales are flat, morale is declining, customers keep leaving, and we keep going over budget on our projects. Yet everyone is frantically busy. The key to good results is the *right* activity and the *right* allocation of resources, not just keeping busy.

Poor performance is rarely the result of a lack of effort. Often, it is the result of spending time and money on activities or strategies that do not add value to the organization. In other words, the actions do not lead to results. Successful organizations that know how to move the needles on their performance gauges do the following:

- Hire the best and brightest people and figure out how to keep them.
- Avoid time-wasting management fads and programs.
- Buy the best tools and resources you can afford.
- Focus on outcomes rather than behavior or effort.
- Link improvement initiatives to strategic plans.
- Build trusting relationships with customers and suppliers.
- Communicate openly and honestly with employees and others.
- Stick with proven techniques until they work—and never give up.
- Focus on consequences to drive human performance.

Moving it does take time, money, people, and effort. Smart organizations have figured out how to get results with minimum effort and resources.

M O V E I T

Beware of Management Fads with Three-Letter Acronyms

Remember TQM? How about SPC, ABC, BSC, and CPI? These programs all looked good at the time, promising to solve all your problems while making the consultants and trainers rich. When I was working with Bell Atlantic, I remember meeting the guy who wrote the "reengineering book." He told me that he did not do consulting anymore because he could not charge enough per day to make it worthwhile. Rather, he conducts public workshops and charges attendees $2,000 each for a three-day session. He said he regularly gets 200 to 300 people in each session. Do the math on that one and it comes out to $400,000 to $600,000 for three days of work! Not a bad gig. Re-engineering was the fad du jour for a couple of years, and the consultants who cashed in on this made their millions and probably quietly retired to Hawaii. You don't hear anything about reengineering today do you?

It's funny how short a memory many organizations seem to have when it comes to management fads. Too many consultants take the old stuff, repackage it so it looks new, put a new name and acronym on it, and then big organizations buy up the programs. Every organization pretty much embraced the TQM movement in the 1990s. Unfortunately, while everyone was forming teams, drawing fishbone diagrams, and eliminating defects, important things like profits were often forgotten. Now, some consultants have repackaged the old TQM methodology, which no one wants anymore, and called it lean manufacturing or six sigma, and clients are buying the stuff up just like they did the old TQM programs fifteen years ago. The good

thing about these management programs is that the people in organizations are mostly new after 15 to 20 years because of turnover and
retirements, so there is a whole new market of clients for this information.

Are all of these management programs a waste of money and
time? Certainly not. Every single one of them involve some valuable approaches that actually have been proven to work to save
costs, boost profits, and build more loyalty from customers. One
problem with all of these management programs is that the benefits
are oversold. None of them are a panacea for all your ills. If you are
in the wrong business at the wrong time, or have problems like lying
and cheating executives—no balanced scorecard, strategic plan, or
six-sigma initiative is going to save you. Good performance always
involves a multitude of efforts all finely tuned and aligned—not a
single program.

The second and more common reason these management programs fail is that organizations do not implement them properly and
provide adequate resources. Executives like the concepts and ideas
but always want to know how they can do it on the cheap. "Can you
cut three days of training down to a half a day?" "Can we get this
up and running in a year rather than the three years you recom-
mend?" "What can we get for 25 percent of that cost?" Any of these
improvement initiatives do work to improve results, but they most
often fail because of a lack of top management support and a lack
of resources.

If your organization is considering any management program or
performance improvement initiative, consider these guidelines:
- Be realistic about the kind of results that will be achieved.
- Don't cut corners on costs and time—either do it right or don't
  do it.
- Think about how you are going to convince skeptical employees that this is not yet another short-lived fad that will go out
  of favor in a few years.
- Whatever program you select, stay with it long enough to see
  the benefits rather than search for a new panacea.

MOVE IT

- Check with other companies who are several years down the road in implementation to see if the promised results materialized.

All of these management programs contain a certain amount of nonsense, a certain amount of common sense, and some excellent techniques that really work to improve performance. See if you can pick out the worthwhile stuff and make it work for your organization.

How to Move It: Do What's Important
❑ **Don't fall into the trap of buying into a management program just because it has a new, important-sounding acronym.** Some can definitely improve productivity or quality and reduce costs. But you can't view them as an automatic panacea, because many of these "new" programs are really just old ideas repackaged, and many are passing fads.
❑ **Do carefully consider your specific needs and whether the new program will meet them.** In other words, do your homework before embarking on what could be a costly and time-consuming effort.

**M
O
V
E

I
T**

Perseverance Is the Key to Success—But Don't Be Stupid About It

A hard lesson to learn in life is when to give up, versus when to keep trying, The high school athlete learns by her senior year that she is probably not going to become a tennis pro. The kid playing in the rock band at weddings and bar mitzvahs realizes by age twenty-five that he is probably not going to become a rock star. After failing to break $10 million in sales five years in a row, the struggling software company finally figures out that it is not going to be the next Microsoft. We all know people who refuse to give up on their dreams, even though everyone around them knows it ain't going to happen—the actress still working as a waitress at Applebee's at age 33 while getting extra work and bit parts in B movies, the 40-year-old volleyball player looking to make a comeback in the biggest tournament of the year, and the middle manager who still thinks the company will realize her brilliance and promote her to vice president some day.

It's sad to see people chasing a dream that the rest of us know is out of their reach. However, as one of my wise southern clients explains, "Even a blind squirrel finds a nut every now and then." Organizations sometimes refuse to give up on their dreams as well, even when they are clearly unrealistic. I run into a number of organizations that come up with vision statements that are so out of touch with reality that they must have been concocted in a haze of marijuana smoke. It's good to have a dream, but it's okay to change your dream when you figure out that it is unachievable.

When you listen to successful people, read about successful organizations, or study the companies that Jim Collins studied in his excellent book *Good to Great* (2002), one theme comes through loud and clear. They all failed many times, but they never gave up and they learned from their failures. Donald Trump has been bankrupt several times, but he always comes back. Madonna comes out with a horrible CD that gets panned by critics and consumers, and she reinvents herself and comes out with a major hit a year later and is all over the news.

I've written a lot more books than I have had published, and I have published a couple of books that I get negative royalty checks on—the publisher makes me pay back an advance that it gave me if the book does not sell. Man, that's depressing when you've already spent the advance check. But I've also written a couple of books that have earned me enough money in royalties to buy a new car every year with cash if I wanted to. When I write a new book or come up with a new workshop and it bombs, I go back and start rewriting it—I don't give up. Now, if I had written ten books and never had one published, I might want to find a different career. Don't give up, but don't be stupid either.

Every successful organization has had many failures. In fact, one organization I worked with had a banquet each year where they give out trophies for the biggest failures of the year. There are different categories of awards, such as worst new product, biggest loser customer we brought onboard, and biggest waste-of-time management initiative. The organization celebrates failures and encourages failures because it believes that if it is not failing it is not taking risks, and it knows that with each failure comes valuable lessons to pass on to others. This approach works like a charm, and the organization has had more home-run successes because taking risks, failing, communicating lessons learned, and applying that knowledge to create success.

Perseverance is one of those values that is hard to teach and goes against human nature. Our natural tendency is to give up and try a different path if the one we're on leads to a dead end. Smart organizations look to hire people who have this value of perseverance. A history of overcoming adversity and constant effort is a good quality to look for in a new employee. The culture of the organization needs to be designed to reinforce this value as well. Sadly, many organizations have a short attention span and do not reward perseverance, but they always seem to be looking for the next new thing. Organizations that follow Winston Churchill's advice and "Never give up" are the ones that win the race.

How to Move It: Do What's Important

❏ *Don't give up on improving your organization.* This doesn't mean that you should chase unrealistic dreams, but if you persevere, sometimes that perseverance pays off. Just set realistic goals.

❏ *Do learn from your mistakes.* Perseverance doesn't mean doing the same thing over and over again if that approach is failing. It does mean trying something new, going down a different path, or taking a different approach to solving a problem. Recognize your failures and celebrate them, because they represent something ventured, but look at them critically to find out what went wrong so you don't make the same mistake again.

**M
O
V
E
I
T**

Minimize Distractions

One of the biggest killers of productivity is being distracted while you are trying to get something done. Some people are good multi-taskers and can do things like talk on the phone and respond to e-mails at the same time. Most work tasks do require a certain amount of concentration, and many people I know are not good multitaskers. Many jobs today involve constant interruptions, but organizations don't seem to put much thought into how to design jobs and tasks for maximum efficiency. Technology has served to make matters worse. Now we can be interrupted via pagers, cell phones, and personal communication devices.

Several of my clients have attempted to get a handle on distractions by creating a measure that goes on everyone's scorecard. It's called the "Distraction Index." The measure does not track day-to-day interruptions, but rather tracks how people spend major chunks of their time. Each week, people fill out a time sheet and sort their time into three categories:

- Job tasks (e.g., engineering, sales, customer services, or whatever)
- Administration (budgets, staff meetings, required training, etc.)
- Management programs (six sigma, Baldrige, strategic planning, etc.)

What several clients found after collecting data for six months is that most employees were spending about two-thirds of their time performing administrative tasks or participating in management programs. Even individual contributors and first-line supervisors were spending far too little time doing what they were hired to do.

Targets were set to have most employees spend two-thirds of their time doing their job and one-third spread across the other categories of activities. The data from the Distraction Index provided the ammunition they needed to start cutting out administrative tasks that added no value, and start minimizing the number of management programs or initiatives that took the valuable time of employees. In eliminating programs and administrative requirements there were hard battles to be fought. The people who were responsible for these programs all believed that they were necessary and important, and should not be cut. Senior management had to get involved and decide which programs or initiatives were going to be eliminated, reduced, modified, or left the same. Many meetings took place, and there was much posturing, politicking, and arguing going on.

In the end, a number of management programs were cut, others were reduced in scope, and a few of the more important initiatives were kept the same. Administrative requirements were also reduced, and processes were improved or simplified to reduce the time employees must spend on these tasks.

In small organizations, everyone must perform multiple jobs and be the salesperson, accountant, manager, and worker. In a large organization, big groups of people do administrative tasks, along with management initiatives such as strategic planning and process improvement. Individually, these initiatives and administrative requirements all look valid and important. When the time requirements for all these things are added up, it becomes a big problem for many employees. You look at the calendars of many managers and find that their time is often spent in back-to-back meetings. Many of the meetings have little to do with the managers' primary responsibilities.

M
O
V
E
I
T

One of the biggest opportunities for improving performance in organizations is to clear out as much of the stuff as possible that distracts people from doing their jobs. This does not mean improving administrative processes for the administrative folks. What it means is minimizing the time that employees must spend on these tasks. Similarly, someone that has the authority and objectivity needs to lay out all the improvement initiatives and management programs and look for overlap, waste, and opportunities to reduce the amount of time people spend on these programs. This way, they can focus most of their attention on doing what they were hired to do in the first place.

How to Move It: Do What's Important

❏ *Don't allow yourself or your employees get distracted from the jobs they were hired to do.* Too many workers spend too much time on administrative tasks instead of the actual, results-oriented work they should be focusing on. Don't let the process get in the way of the product or service you're trying to provide efficiently.

❏ *Do find out where your people are spending most of their time.* Determine what the distractions are by tracking them for a while. Then do everything you can to get rid of them, if possible, or at least minimize the time required to respond to them. Make sure your people are focusing on the work that's *really* important to the success of your organization.

M O V E   I T

Activity Does Not Equal Results

Managers always feel better when they see people who look busy and engaged in work. An office worker friend explains that she always takes a file folder or two with her and always walks fast. As a result, people think she is a hard worker even though she confesses to only working about three hours out of an eight-hour day. Many slackers have learned the right behaviors to spend time on to give the impression that they are hardworking team players. Most eventually get found out, but some have managed to slack off their entire careers by engaging in some shrewd behaviors. The point of this chapter is that *moving it* is about getting results, not about behavior or action. In the same way that people write many goals and plans that they never achieve, they also waste a lot of time on activities that do nothing to produce results.

You see this at work, at play, and in all activities. I watch people sweating in the gym, doing exercises all wrong, lifting heavy weights, and they wonder why they never look any different. The best lesson I got in finding the right behaviors to spend time on and deciding which should be dropped from my repertoire was a recent client project. A large industrial organization hired me to help determine the core competencies of Project Supervisor. This was one of the top jobs in the company, and Project Supervisors managed projects with budgets of more than $50 million that involved hundreds and even thousands of people.

My project involved studying the two top performers—Frank and Billy—and contrasting them with the poor- or average-per-

forming Project Supervisors to find the difference. They all had similar educations, similar prior experience, and strong dedication to
the organization. When I studied the poor- and average-performing
supervisors, I found that they all:

- Worked more than seventy hours every week
- Received thirty to forty phone calls per day
- Received seventy-five to one hundred e-mails per day
- Were well liked by their peers and subordinates
- Participated in company teams and improvement initiatives
- Felt stressed out by the job

With all this effort and behavior, these Project Supervisors were
consistently way over budget on projects, missed major milestones,
and had a lot of rework and defects on their projects.

Billy and Frank's projects were always major successes. They
were done under budget, on time or early, and often with close to
zero defects. These two guys were legendary in their ability to
achieve good results, yet their behavior would lead you to think they
were not hard workers. Frank explained it to me in an interview:

**M
O
V
E
I
T**

> My priorities are my health, my family, and my job, in that
> order. I never come in before 7:30 and leave every day at
> 4:30. I work out at the gym until 5:45, shower, and have din-
> ner with my wife and kids each night at 6:30. I never work
> weekends because that is when I spend time with my family.
> I don't read e-mails, so people don't send them to me. I don't
> participate in any committees or any of the B.S. manage-
> ment programs they have going on here, and I tell my man-
> agers to only call me with something they shouldn't be
> handling on their own, so I only get three or four phone calls
> a day. I also don't bother with that stupid five-pound time
> management notebook everyone lugs around. I know what's
> important and I get it done, rather than spend an hour a day
> writing down all this stuff.

As you might expect, lots of people resent Frank and think he is
arrogant (he is), but Frank and his counterpart Billy have full lives
outside of work and do not appear stressed out like the poor per-

formers. Maybe Frank and Billy are just smarter than their peers, but I don't think so. I think that both of these guys have learned which behaviors are important and which ones are not. The lesson here is that the hardest-working, busiest people are often the worst performers. Study the ones who are calm, relaxed, and go home at 5:00 while producing incredible results, and you will start to understand that a lot of the behavior managers see that makes them feel better is probably a waste of time.

How to Move It: Do What's Important

❏ ***Don't let your employees get caught up in looking busy but not getting any real work accomplished.*** This is another easy trap to fall into, and many employees even take advantage of it. But just because someone's on the phone (even with a co-worker) or answering e-mail or going to meetings doesn't mean that person is doing important work that results in something tangible.

❏ ***Do look at your most successful and happiest employees to find out what they do that others could adopt.*** It's not necessary to reinvent the wheel, just find out how your wheels work best and then emulate that behavior, if possible. If there's something that's getting in the way of getting the job done, do everything you can to eliminate that activity—or find someone else to do it who can do it faster, more efficiently, or better. Make sure your best people have the time and energy needed to get their real jobs done.

**M
O
V
E

I
T**

Limit Process Improvement Teams and Projects

Total quality management and quality circles were popular in the late 1980s and 1990s. These approaches have morphed into similar initiatives called six sigma or lean management, which involved getting people together on teams to diagnose the causes of problems and to work on solutions. I remember working with an aerospace client in suburban Boston in 1993 that had every single employee on one or more process improvement teams. The company lost a major customer that accounted for about one-third of its business during that time frame because of quality problems. Another client went from profitability to Chapter 11 while everyone was on a team drawing process models and fishbone diagrams. I was hired as an expert witness in a lawsuit against the CEO and consultant who were both fired.

The problem wasn't the fact that teams were trying to improve processes—that really is a good thing. The problem was that there were way too many teams and projects. People were spending so much time getting training and participating in team meetings that regular work like taking care of customers did not get done. The company that went Chapter 11 was a car dealership with sixteen dealerships. A sales manager I spoke with explained: "People came on the lot looking at the cars and eventually left because no one was there to help them—they were all in team meetings!"

A smarter way to improve the way work is done or processed is to limit the number of projects to between three and ten in any given year. One Baldrige Award-winning company picked ten improvement projects per year that it called its "Ten Most Wanted." This was a much smarter approach. Another client limited its improvement efforts to about six each year. Each one was linked to a major goal in the strategic plan, and teams were staffed with some of the best people and provided with the resources they needed (time, money, equipment, and people) to be successful.

Another client achieved great success by working on the one major improvement initiative per year that was needed by most business units. One year everyone worked on improving the planning process. Another year they worked on developing balanced performance metrics. Supplier management was a process that was improved another year. The company has had more than 100 years of profitable growth by getting a lot better at one thing each year.

The point of this chapter is that improving performance involves studying key work processes to find ways to perform them better or faster or cheaper. However, organizations have lots of real work that has to be done each year to pay the bills. The real work should always come first and be the priority. Process improvement is something that you spend a small amount of time doing each year. Pick a few processes to improve that are either broken, or where there is vast opportunity for improvement.

The best approaches I've seen to process improvement do involve teams and a process like six sigma. However, the process for selecting the improvement projects is more important than the process used to analyze and improve the projects. It begins by setting a goal such as "improve market share" or "reduce manufacturing costs." In order to achieve the goal, processes need to be identified, studied, and selected for improvement. There are often many ways to achieve a goal, so the overall strategy must first be selected. Let's say you decided that the best strategy for gaining market share is to get more business from your existing big customers. This would mean that the key account-selling or customer-relationship-building process would be the one selected for analysis and improvement.

Each goal in your strategic plan should be the impetus for a possible process improvement initiative. It may be that a goal can be achieved without a team or process improvement initiative. For example, a strategy for improving market share might be to buy a competitor. Often, however, achieving goals does involve improving work processes. Just make sure that you limit your improvements to a few a year so as not to distract yourself from your day-to-day work.

How to Move It: Do What's Important

❑ ***Don't let process improvements get in the way of real work.*** Many organizations get so caught up in setting up teams or projects to improve the way they do things that they lose sight of the real work that needs to get done to satisfy customers and pay the bills. Don't let this happen to you: Improve your processes, but allocate a sensible amount of time and people for these projects.

❑ ***Do pick a few important processes that need improvement and focus on one or just a few of these at a time.*** Once you've achieved one or several process goals—while meeting your primary goals regarding the products or services your organization provides—then you can move on to the next one. Prioritizing is critical—and so much easier than tackling everything at once.

MOVE IT

Benchmarking Is Often an Excuse for Corporate Field Trips

Remember when it used to be considered wrong or at least a sign of weakness to steal ideas from other companies and implement them on your own? Not anymore, stealing ideas is now called benchmarking. I've noticed that there are a lot more benchmarking trips going on in the winter in Florida and California than other places at other times of the year. Benchmarking has become, in many instances, an opportunity to go somewhere warm and fun like Orlando and tell your boss you're going to benchmark the best practices of Disney. Staying at a Ritz Carlton for a few nights in New York and Dana Point might also be considered benchmarking, since the Ritz has many good practices and has won two Baldrige Awards.

Benchmarking is a practice first noticed in the early 1990s as being practiced by a few pioneering firms like Xerox, one of the first Baldrige Award winners. The idea is that you can get some great ideas for improving processes by studying other companies that perform with much greater efficiency or at lower cost than you do. There is sound logic to this approach, and a number of organizations have saved many dollars and hours of time by simply implementing the best practices of others. Benchmarking can be an excellent way of shortcutting process improvement by letting other companies do the trial and error until they hit on an approach that works. For the cost of a three-day trip for a couple of your people, you go for a visit, copy a company's approach, and get immediate improvement.

Like most business breakthroughs, however, benchmarking did not work so well for a lot of companies. The best-run companies found themselves besieged by others who wanted to come and benchmark their best practices. One company I worked with had to make a rule that said: "You are welcome to come benchmark one of our processes if you have a best practice that we want to benchmark. If you are just a mediocre firm looking to get free ideas from us— look elsewhere. We have a business to run." This might sound a little mean and selfish, but the company was running tour groups through facilities every week, distracting employees, causing accidents, and hurting productivity. Back when Saturn was a most admired company, it started charging $5,000 for a benchmarking visit. I heard they were making more money on running tours than on the cars themselves.

Another problem with benchmarking is that many of the companies that you find in benchmarking databases are a legend in their own minds. They often volunteer that they have great practices that others should copy, but there is often no verification or proof given. A client of mine went to visit a company that was in the benchmark database for its HR practices and said the company's approach to human resources was generic and outdated. (My client suggested that the company come visit him, to see better HR practices.) Do a lot of phone calling and Internet research on potential companies to benchmark before ever buying an airplane ticket. Make sure the organization you are going to visit really has a best practice to study.

The final problem with benchmarking is lack of focus and preparation. Benchmarking should focus on a singular goal and process, such as improving contractor management, hiring, or customer satisfaction measurement. Once a process has been selected, you need to create a plan for how the time will be spent and identify the data that is needed. People often return from a benchmarking trip and later realize they failed to gather a lot of detail that the team back home needs.

Like most management fads, benchmarking is a process that can be very useful and effective, but it is more often neither one. The key to making it work is proper planning, focus, detailed data collection, and making sure that the benchmarking partner you pick is, in fact, as good as it claims. Great companies all have their best practices, as well as some processes that you would never want to benchmark. Some of the best companies to benchmark are often not the big corporations that are always in the news. They are the small and medium-sized organizations that you have never heard of. Also keep in mind that a lot of benchmarking can be done via telephone, Internet, and e-mail.

How to Move It: Do What's Important

❑ *Don't benchmark other companies until you're sure your company will benefit from the exercise.* Employees at some companies go on "benchmarking trips" that are really corporate boondoggles—a lot of fun for the employees on the trip, but not much payoff for the company footing the bill. Other organizations benchmark companies they think will offer some insight on how to do something better only to learn nothing useful at all. Don't wander down the wrong path when looking for a new road to success.

❑ *Do research other companies that are "best practice" organizations, especially in the specific area in which you need help.* This is a useful way to emulate your competition or comparable companies: if you have a specific goal, know what you're looking for, and have some reason to believe that this specific company can help you, then move on it!

M
O
V
E
I
T

Beware of Solutions in Search of Problems

Remember the story about the kid with a toy hammer who sees the whole world as a nail? Well, adults seem to have the same problem. A few years ago, every new company had the letter *e* in its name. "E-business" this and "e-business" that showed the world that they were ready to do business on the Web. Everyone I talked to had an idea for an Internet start-up. Luckily, most of them kept their day jobs. People saw the Internet as a tool that would revolutionize the way that all business is done. Most of those e-business companies have gone out of business, and only a few, such as eBay and Amazon, have managed to become successful and even profitable. The Internet was a solution in search of an application. It did have some excellent uses, just as a hammer does, but it is a tool and nothing more.

For a while I held off getting a Web site, but I finally broke down and had my brother build me one a couple of years ago. I get an average of 2,000 hits a month, which sounds like a lot to me, but I don't think I have gotten one dollar of paying work from someone who visited my Web site. Maybe my picture scares them away— should have gotten more airbrushing.

I see all sorts of organizations that get enamored with some new tool or approach and after buying it go out in search of opportunities to use it. One client fell in love with activity-based costing, or ABC. They trained a small army of ABC practitioners who went out in search of processes on which to perform ABC analyses. Each facility had a full-time ABC coordinator, and there were many ABC teams performing these complicated and time-consuming analyses, which often resulted in minimal savings.

Another client became enamored with lean manufacturing and in the first few years saw dramatic improvements in cycle time, costs, and productivity in its warehouses and manufacturing facilities. When it tried to apply the approach to service and support organizations, the improvements were scant or nonexistent.

Tools like the Internet, ABC, lean manufacturing, six sigma, and the like have helped thousands of organizations in many ways, but they are just tools and not solutions to all problems. I encourage my clients to be skeptics when it comes to some new tool or approach (except the ones that I happen to be selling, of course). Just like that thing you bought from a TV infomercial at 2 A.M. never worked the way the ad promised on TV, organizations get sold snake oil as well. The biggest reason this is such a common problem is that we buy the solution without first having a specific problem or goal. We read a new management book, hear a presentation at a conference, sit next to a guy on an airplane, or read an article in *Business Week* or the *Wall Street Journal* about some new tool, technique, or program, and we think we have to have it.

The salesperson comes in with a slick dog-and-pony show, extolling all the benefits of this new tool, and listing all the big-name companies that have had it for over a year, and you're ready to buy today.

Often, this love affair with a new tool or technique ends with the reality of how much work the new software, or whatever it is, takes to implement. Years later, you may still be working on the conversion and end up spending much more than you had originally planned.

M
O
V
E
I
T

How to Move It: Do What's Important

❑ ***Don't just follow the crowd on the latest management fad.*** The "next new solution" may not offer any benefit for your business if it's not solving a problem you actually have. Don't be a lemming: Remember, they all ran off a cliff and drowned.

❑ ***Do be proactive to avoid buying unnecessary tools and searching for problems or applications that the "new solution" can solve.*** First, identify your problems or goals: Then go out in search of a tool that might solve the problem or allow you to achieve the goal. Once again, improvement initiatives should be driven by the strategic plan, not some slick sales pitch or article you read. Second, challenge the claims of the tool salespeople and check with other customers whose judgment you trust. Make sure that all those you check with are beyond the honeymoon phase so you get the real story on the long-term usefulness of a tool or application.

M
O
V
E

I
T

Don't Get Creative When Landing the Plane

One thing we learned from the quality movement that survived the death of the TQM fad is the importance of consistency in the way work is done. Processes need to be documented, standards set, and controls put in place to ensure that things are done the same way each time. Organizations like fast-food businesses are masters of process control so that you get the same impersonal service and mediocre food at any one of their 8,500 locations around the world. Process control is easy if you can keep human mistakes out of the work process as much as possible. I have worked with several large paper companies and the aluminum manufacturer Alcoa. These companies have process control down to a finely tuned science. They monitor input variables, use computer-controlled equipment to monitor process variables, and adjust factors like speed, pressure, and force when necessary to ensure that the end product turns out the same way every time.

Most work processes today have a lot of human behavior in them and can't be automated like the paper or aluminum plant. When you have human behavior, special care must be taken to get consistent work processes. Airlines land thousands of flights per day without a problem, and this is a fairly difficult task, given factors like weather and the many other aircraft that want to land at around the same time at the same airport. Yet it is performed almost perfectly day after day. There is no mystery why this is done so well. All the elements of a flawless process control system exist. First of all, pilots are screened for their mental and physical abilities. They also

M
O
V
E

I
T

receive excellent training, when they begin and in each successive year. Cockpits have been designed by human factors engineers to provide all the important information in an easy-to-see format. On each flight, pilots have checklists to complete, and there is usually a copilot. There is also something else that ensures process control—consequences. Pilots who make mistakes when landing a 777 might not live to fly another day.

Many work tasks are like landing a plane. There is one right way to do it, and it is important to perform all the right steps in the exact same sequence every single time. There are a number of work processes in organizations that are not like landing a plane, however. Process control using checklists, standards, feedback, and controls for these tasks often work as a detriment in an organization. Processes that involve any sort of imagination or creativity do not lend themselves well to process control. Solving problems, teaching, designing software, marketing, sales, writing, and creating music, a film, or ad campaign are all tasks or processes that require some degree of creativity. In all of them, there is a basic process to follow.

But following a process does not guarantee success, like when you are landing a plane. A filmmaker can employ all the techniques used by successful filmmakers in the past and have a film bomb at the box office. A teacher can follow a lesson plan and teach exactly what is in the book, and the kids can be bored to death and not remember the lesson long enough to pass a test at the end of the week. A health care professional can follow a standard series of diagnostic tests and still fail to detect the real cause of a patient's problem.

If any of your work processes require some degree of creativity and there is more than one right way to do something, you need a different approach to process management. They key here is to first make sure not to overengineer a process by requiring employees to blindly follow a series of steps. A process like sales is more of an art than a science. Nordstrom teaches sales associates a few basic steps but encourages them to use their brains and tailor their approach to each customer. Other service companies prefer to hire people without much in the way of brains, and then give them scripts and checklists and supervise the hell out of them to make sure they perform right.

Process control is possible for creative work to some degree. You can learn the most important aspects of a creative process by closely studying your best performers. Their behavior will give clues as to what they do that makes them more successful than their peers. If the work process is more mental, you can get the master performers to talk through the thought processes and document these for others. Organizations that outperform their competitors have very different approaches for controlling repetitive and creative work processes. Make sure you do not have a "one size fits all" approach to your work processes.

How to Move It: Do What's Important

❑ *Don't standardize the wrong functions.* Some processes should follow a series of very specific, strictly controlled steps for maximum productivity and efficiency—but some shouldn't. Identify those in your organization that should and make sure your employees are following your rules, guidelines, and procedures on these specific processes.

❑ *Do recognize which functions are more art than science.* In your organization, these might include sales presentations, customer service, product design, or other creative activities. Just make sure your employees know which these are so that they can be flexible in how they handle those processes.

**M
O
V
E
I
T**

Buy the Best Tools
You Can Afford

One of the smartest consultants I've ever met was Tom Gilbert, whose 1978 book, *Human Competence*, is the best book I've ever read on improving organizational performance. Tom was a big believer in focusing on results as opposed to behavior. Performance is made up of the process, or behavior, and the accomplishment. The accomplishment is the finished product or the closed deal, while the behavior, or process, is the work involved in producing the accomplishment. Many organizations foolishly manage the process or behavior measures even when they fail to predict successful accomplishments. Sales managers grill their associates until they can do a demo word-for-word from the script with all the correct hand motions. Yet the woman who refuses to follow the script closes more deals than her peers who follow the script to the letter.

Often, the difference between exemplary and mediocre performance is a better tool, not harder work or following a process. The productivity of rental car return clerks must have improved by 1,000 percent when they were given handheld bar code readers and receipt printers. My friend who recently got a DSL line claims to work about an hour less per day because information he needs can be accessed so quickly.

The right tools can make a huge difference in what employees can accomplish. Keep in mind the warning in a previous chapter about the kid with the hammer; however, the right tool can often do more to improve performance and produce results than any process improvement effort. I watch people in meetings redrawing the boxes on the flowchart of some convoluted process when the use of a good tool might eliminate the need for the process altogether. Imagine the people at Avis trying to figure out how to reduce the time it takes to check in a returning rental car customer and give him a receipt. They probably did not even think that some technology might allow people to return cars and get a receipt in about a minute, without even going in to the counter.

A question that should be thoroughly explored in each initiative designed to improve performance is: "Could we buy some tool or device that would dramatically improve our performance?" This obvious question is rarely asked in meetings designed to analyze and improve work processes. I've sat in on many of these meetings and watched people move around boxes on the flowcharts and change the sequence of subprocesses, only to later realize that the improvements in performance were minimal. I would encourage process and performance improvement teams to exhaust all possibilities of tools that might aid in improving performance before even thinking of changing their existing process.

Once you identify that there might be some hardware, software, or other type of tool that would improve performance, don't get the bargain basement version. Quality is remembered long after price is forgotten, but if the procurement people get involved, you can bet that the lowest price will be a desirable option. A few organizations I work with make it a point to always buy the best tools and equipment they can possibly afford. This is a hard lesson to learn, but an important one. My friend Lee always buys a new Mercedes every three to four years. A military client, with whom I have done many projects, looked for the best-balanced scorecard software product to use for their organization. As with all major purchases in the government, they had to go out and get bids. Well, they received bids that ranged from about $20,000 up to over $200,000. After much study and a clarification of their requirements and needs, they ended up buying one of the most expensive products. It did everything they needed it to do, was easy to navigate, had excellent graphics, and saved them enough money in not having to prepare charts for meetings that it paid for itself in less than a year. Another client took the cheap route and bought the $20,000 software that on the surface looked similar to the more expensive packages. No one uses it, and they are still spending hundreds of hours each month preparing PowerPoint charts for meetings.

Often, the right tools can dramatically improve performance. Buy the best you can possibly afford—it will be cheaper in the long run.

How to Move It: Do What's Important

❑ *Don't work harder, work smarter.* Okay, it's a cliché, but the reason it's cliché is that it's true. Don't keep banging your head against the wall, trying to make incremental improvements in some process. Instead, consider whether there's a completely different approach or tool you can use to cut through your Gordian knot.

❑ *Do get the best tools possible for the specific job at hand.* Whether it's equipment or new technology, the right tool can make a huge difference in productivity, efficiency, and employee morale. If the job can be done easier and faster, your staff will be happier—and obviously get more done.

MOVE IT

Hire the Best Versus Train the Rest

Corporate universities came into fashion in the 1980s as organizations found they needed to develop a new crop of leaders as older ones began to retire. The military and government got into the training and development business in a big way in the last ten years when they looked at an aging federal workforce that would leave a gaping hole in skills and competencies when they all walk out the door. Succession planning, training, and development are all good things if done right, but they rarely are.

One of the most important factors in your success is bringing in the right talent in the first place and placing it in the right jobs. Jim Collins calls this "getting the right people on the bus." It's hard enough to get the right people, but a bigger challenge is making sure they are on the right bus. I run across many organizations that have hired bright hardworking people and placed them in the wrong jobs. They hire brilliant engineers and make them managers when they are good at being engineers. Most engineers I know don't get too passionate about dealing with people or administrative issues, which is the main job of a manager. What they get off on is working on technical issues, solving problems, or doing analyses. They often hate dealing with people issues and are often not very good at it.

Getting the right person in the right job can do more to improve performance or move the needles on your corporate dashboard than just about any other single action. I witnessed this at a federal employer with which I have worked on and off for many years. The site has about 500 employees and 5,000 contractors who do most of the day-to-day work. This particular group of federal employees did support work like HR, contracts, and procurement. It was about the most despondent group I've worked with. Many explained their jobs as "white collar welfare." The boss of the group retired, and the site brought in a new manager from headquarters in Washington, D.C. Brent did not have much of a background in HR, contracts, or any of the other functions he was overseeing, but he was rumored to be a good manager.

It turned out that Brent was about the best manager I've met in twenty-five years of consulting. In about six months, Brent took this unmotivated, unproductive, unhappy group and turned it into a high-performance team. The things he did were pretty simple, but they worked. He had each department work to eliminate tasks that did not add value, he made extensive use of praise, celebration, and other forms of positive reinforcement, and he made people feel like their jobs really mattered. What was so cool about this is that Brent really loved being a manger. He had passion for his job and loved dealing with the people issues that confront managers. He was also excellent at knocking out roadblocks that prevented his people from being productive.

I've not run across many Brent's in organizations with whom I've consulted. This one person did more to move performance from negative to positive in more areas than anything else the other organizations could have done. They see managers like Brent and think that they can clone them with the right leadership program or corporate university. The problem with this approach is that most who attend these programs will never become a Brent; nor do many of them have a passion for the job as Brent did.

The resources that organizations devote to developing their people is often ten times what they spend selecting them and placing them in the right position. My experience is that the selection process is vastly more important, and when done properly has the biggest impact on performance. Mayer Electric, a little company I worked with in Birmingham, Alabama, realized this. It has a program called Success by Selection, which is a long and expensive process of sorting through job candidates to find just the right person to fill each position. My client told me that Mayer courted him for about six months of interviews, tests, trips to assessment centers, and simulations before they eventually offered him a job.

If you want to achieve impressive results, pay a lot more attention to the people you pick and the jobs you place them in, rather than trying to develop and train everyone.

How to Move It: Do What's Important

❏ *Don't promote talented workers into the wrong jobs.* Too many organizations unwittingly follow The "Peter Principle": They move their most skilled workers up into positions they're not qualified for—and that many don't even want! This is an easy trap to fall into. Review your employees' strengths and weaknesses carefully before moving them out of a position in which they're excelling.

❏ *Do appoint the right people by fully understanding the skills and experience needed for each position.* If you need a strong manager, hire someone with management skills, which sounds ridiculously obvious, but isn't. Make sure the person has managed what you need them to manage: A project? A team? It's easier to hire right the first time than to train people to make up for what they're lacking.

**M
O
V
E

I
T**

Accountability and Consequences

Just about every client I've worked with in the last five years claims to have a problem with accountability, or a lack thereof. One client even listed improving accountability as its number one goal in its current strategic plan. It formed a team to address the issue, and the team struggled for about three months to agree on what is meant by the term *accountability*.

Accountability means people do what they are supposed to do, what you hired them to do. The accountability team tossed around many ideas for improving accountability and decided that the best way was to have the senior leaders make an inspirational talking head video that would motivate the employees to be more accountable. Everyone watched the video, and a year later accountability still made the short list as one of the biggest problems and most important goal for improvement.

If you have a problem with accountability in your organization, nine times out of ten it is due to an imbalance of consequences. People generally know what they are expected to do and usually get some sort of feedback; it's just that they are allowed to get away with doing what Homer Simpson says every red-blooded American worker does every day: "a half-assed job." In the industrial organization that I mentioned, good workers who do their jobs well get requested to work on projects by managers, are always busy, and generally get rewarded with more work. Those who slack off sit around in a group called excess labor and wait for someone to assign them to a project. If they screw up badly enough (which they usually do), the manager never requests them again or makes sure to give them assignments that they can't possibly screw up. Good performance is punished; poor performance is rewarded.

In most organizations, you can get disciplined or fired if you screw up often enough or badly enough, but this almost never happens in either industry or government. One bold manager fired a habitually poor performer who had been disciplined many times and he went to the union and got his job back. So, the manger was punished for even trying to deal with poor performance.

In organizations where there is a high degree of accountability, the following characteristics can be found:

- Job responsibilities are clear with little overlap between departments and positions.
- Measures of performance and targets have been identified for each job.
- Employees receive regular (e.g., monthly) feedback on their job performance.
- Good performance is rewarded and poor performance is punished.

I have run into a number of organizations that have mastered the first three points. They have clear position descriptions, clearly defined roles and responsibilities for departments, scorecards and targets for each job, and regular feedback on performance measures. What most lack is effective-consequence systems. For consequences to be effective they must be four things:

1. Personal—the individual experiences the consequences, not the organization.
2. Powerful—they need to be strong enough to affect behavior.
3. Immediate—the closer in time they are to the behavior or performance, the more powerful they are.
4. Certain—remote consequences, like getting lung cancer someday, do not control much behavior.

If you look at the consequence systems in most organizations, they lack most of these characteristics. In many companies, it's almost as if they have engineered a system of rewards and punishments to drive poor performance. If there is one thing you can do to improve accountability and performance in your organization, it is not training, team building, goal setting, or any other HR initiative; it is designing positive and negative consequences to drive exceptional performance.

How to Move It: Do What's Important

❏ *Don't let your weak employees get lazy—and don't overwork your best employees.* This happens in many organizations that haven't set clear responsibilities—and results—for their employees. If workers believe they won't be held accountable for meeting goals, they won't worry about or work toward meeting them.

❏ *Do make sure your employees know what's expected of them and give them feedback so they know where they stand.* Employees need to be accountable for their work, and you need to reward your good and great employees and discipline and punish your not-so-great employees.

M O V E   I T

Build Trusting Relationships with Stakeholders

Lying seems to have become the national pastime in America. Everybody lies: your boss, your doctor, your wife, your kids, your preacher, even you! Everyone has told some boldfaced lie and life goes on—people mostly get away with it to lie another day. Many ethics specialists say that dishonesty has become so ingrained in our culture that regulation or prosecution of a few liars is unlikely to do any good. We even have a name for professional liars—they're called spin doctors. Comedian Chris Rock says that men lie the most (pretty much all the time), while women tell the biggest lies.

Everyone you talk to will tell you how important honesty is. Success in organizations is built on relationships, and relationships are built on trust, honesty, and integrity. An important factor in the success of any organization is getting customers and other important stakeholders to trust you. Trust takes a long time to earn and a short time to lose. Catch your husband in a big lie, and those twenty years of trust in your marriage go out the window. Catch your company CEO in a lie and your loyalty to the company changes dramatically in one day.

Salespeople and executives can be the biggest liars, yet they are the ones who have the most responsibility for building trusting relationships with customers, shareholders, and other important groups. Part of building relationships with people involves having fun with them. A software company I work with recently had a big party for its customers as part of the annual user group meeting. Several hundred customers came to New Orleans for a little learning and a lot

M O V E I T

of fun. We went on a riverboat ride with gambling, live music, food, and plenty of alcohol, and then most of the attendees went out late into the night on Bourbon Street for more drinking and partying. Laughing, drinking, eating, and having fun together is a huge part of how relationships are built.

The most important factor about building relationships is not fun, however; it is trust. Trust is built over many experiences with a person or group to see if they demonstrate values like honesty, integrity, and honoring commitments. A company I worked with in Mission Viejo, California years ago was Coldwell Banker Relocation. It worked with big corporations to help its employees move to new cities when they got a promotion or a new assignment. Coldwell Banker had an effort it called Preserving the Trust, which was a systematic approach to building trusting relationships with major corporate customers. Preserving the trust applied to every person in the company, because they all did work that would help in meeting commitments to customers. The company taught everyone from the clerk in the mail room to its top executives about the importance of honesty and honoring commitments to customers and others. Coldwell Banker got to be very good at building relationships over time, and had many long-term customers for whom it did all their relocation work.

Many organizations leave this important process to chance. They trust their account executives or salespeople to do what it takes to bring in new customers and build their trust. But this process of building relationships can be defined, managed, and controlled. Another client, the government lobbying department of a major defense contractor, had a systematic approach for building relationships with key politicians and military leaders. They first identified the most important people to target for support, learned their personal likes and dislikes, and developed a relationship-building strategy tailored to each individual. During each interaction the lobbyists also knew that their character was being judged, so they made sure that they always acted with integrity and followed through on commitments.

MOVE IT

How to Move It: Do What's Important

Two things should be done to improve your ability to create positive relationships with customers and stakeholders:

❏ *Don't tolerate lying or broken promises.* You need to communicate this up front to people, and make quick examples of those who violate the rule by getting rid of them.

❏ *Do develop a planned, systematic approach for establishing and maintaining relationships with customers and others.* And monitor your progress frequently.

**M
O
V
E
I
T**

Use Training Sparingly

Too many accidents this month—we need more safety training. Salespeople not hitting their targets—let's do some more sales training. Leaders not leading the organization properly—send them to a three-day leadership course or, better yet, a two-week executive development program. Catch executives and managers lying and cheating—send them to ethics training. Training seems to be the catchall solution for problems in organizations. We expect it to change behavior and attitudes, motivate, produce results, and communicate. But training cannot do any of these things and is often used inappropriately because it looks like we are taking action if are holding classes.

When a drug company got into trouble with the Food and Drug Administration, part of the consent decree was to hold classes on problem solving for all technical employees and managers. An appliance store was busted for "bait and switch" and was required by a judge to put all salespeople through training on ethics in sales. Training makes us feel like we are doing something to improve performance when, in fact, nothing really changes after most training.

A chain of automotive dealerships spent millions of dollars teaching the quality principles of Dr. Deming to all its employees. A year later, all that most could remember of the training was that it was about some old bald white guy who helped save Japanese industry. The company almost went bankrupt while everyone was in team meetings drawing process models and fishbone diagrams. Another company spent even more millions teaching everyone the habits of successful people and all they could remember a year later was that it was another bald guy who claimed to have seven secrets to success, and some good stories. The company continued to have dismal performance in spite of the fact that everyone had been taught to be successful.

Training can only do one thing—provide someone with knowledge and skills that he or she may have been lacking. The only true test of whether training is needed is to offer someone a million dollars, or hold a gun to his head and tell him to do a job or task. If he cannot do it under threat of death or the promise of being a millionaire, he probably needs training. Once you are certain that a performance problem is not caused by improper consequences, lack of resources, poor job environment, or other factors, only then should you think about doing some training. Ask this question every time someone suggests training is needed. The next important question to ask is: Will this knowledge or skill actually help people perform better on the job? It may be interesting to know the theory of how an automotive engine works, but will it make me a better driver? It's doubtful.

Use training only when you know someone does not know how to do something, and when you are certain that the new knowledge and skills will help improve job performance. Finally, check to make sure the training actually works. Give people a test, don't just ask them if they liked the training and thought it was a fun class. Make sure that whatever test you use is a performance test. Make people fly the plane, not answer ten multiple-choice questions about aviation and weather. There are a lot of incompetent people in professions that have simply given them knowledge tests to certify them.

Think about what you want people to do before you build or buy any training. Make sure people already don't know how to do the things you want and that the new behaviors will really produce results. Finally, make sure that the training includes enough practice for people to master the knowledge and skills they need. Think of all the things in school that you have forgotten—probably 98 percent, right? Yet, most of us still remember the multiplication tables. The reasons are very simple: We practiced them over and over with flash cards until we got them down, and we still use this knowledge in daily life, such as when we have to figure out the tip on a $38 lunch tab.

MOVE IT

Apply these principles to your training and only use them when you are certain they are needed and you will save your organizations millions of dollars in wasted classes that do nothing to help the bottom line.

How to Move It: Do What's Important

❑ **Don't waste your company's valuable time and money on inappropriate training.** Too many organizations think training is a panacea for all problems, but it's not. Too often, it's just busywork that makes managers feel as though they're doing the right thing because they're taking action in a seemingly positive way. Not all training is necessary or helpful.

❑ **Do implement training when people need more knowledge or skills to actually do their jobs.** If the training doesn't help improve their productivity, efficiency, quality of work, or overall job effectiveness, then it's useless. Make sure the training you're investing in is truly useful.

M O V E I T

Ensure Ethics by Balancing Trust and Control

There is a big focus today on ethics and governance in organizations. Every week we read about some new company and its executives who are being accused of illegal or unethical behavior. The Sarbanes-Oxley Act requires executives to review financial results and sign a statement to ensure the integrity of the data. Many organizations have implemented "whistle-blower" programs so that it is easier for employees to report wrongdoings by their employer without retribution. Steps have been taken in many organizations to give more power to boards and other oversight groups, and to ensure their objectivity. Yet experts on corporate culture suggest that these actions are unlikely to solve the ethics crisis in which we now find ourselves.

In earlier chapters, I talked about the importance of defining clear and explicit values and rules so that people know what is expected of them. *Moving it* is about getting behavior to be consistent with the values. In examining how organizations go about this, I rarely see a good balance between trust and control. In most big corporations, there is too much trust, and too much left up to the individual judgment of employees, which has led to major ethical problems. The rules were vague, allowed for multiple interpretations, and there was little policing of employee behavior.

In government organizations, there is very little trust. There are clear and explicit rules for just about every situation, and the rules are very black-and-white—not grey. There are many groups (e.g., inspectors general, auditors, etc.) that police the behavior of employees. No one trusts anyone in government, and employees often feel like there are always six or seven people looking over their work, behavior, e-mails, and everything else. Of course, corruption and unethical behavior is much rarer in many government organizations, but there is a big price to pay for this compliance. Employees are often miserable and resentful that even after twenty years of loyal service to the government, they are not trusted.

Organizations that are known for their integrity and honesty manage to balance trust and control. An organization I worked with that embarked on a successful culture-change initiative began with an assessment of its existing strategies for ensuring ethical behavior. It sorted its programs, strategies, and activities into two categories: Trust and Control.

Trust-Building Strategies

- Training on ethics and values
- Instituting a reward program for ethical behavior
- Screening prospective employees for values
- Communicating examples of ethical behavior
- Modeling ethical behavior
- Fostering empowerment
- Eliminating rules and policies that are too strict
- Decreasing audits and inspections
- Supervising less
- Asking employees for input on rules, policies, and values

Control Strategies

- Audits and inspections
- Whistle-blower programs
- More or stricter rules and policies
- Disciplinary programs
- Covert observation and review
- Increased supervision
- Tighter spans of control
- Stricter penalties for wrongdoers

When many organizations do this sort of assessment, they find that 70 to 80 percent of their efforts and resources are devoted to control strategies, and very little emphasis is placed on trust-building strategies. The appropriate balance is about 50–50.

How to Move It: Do What's Important

❏ ***Don't create a police state with hundreds of rules and "big brother" watching everywhere.*** This isn't the solution to controlling the behavior of employees, although many organizations believe that it is, and they therefore implement too many rules and unwittingly create an environment of fear and mistrust. On the other hand, don't give people guidelines that are too general, and then expect them to do the right thing in all situations.

❏ ***Do create an environment that balances trust and control.*** This requires establishing guidelines, and training and empowering your employees so they know you trust them. But it also involves inspecting, supervising, and disciplining employees so they know there are consequences if they break that trust.

**M
O
V
E
I
T**

Make Employees Look Forward to Coming to Work

Bernard was eligible for retirement three years ago and keeps threatening to retire, but he stays because he still enjoys his job. He has many friends at work, is good at what he does, feels valued, and knows that if he retired he would miss the work and people too much. Anne is worth millions thanks to early investments in company stock, and even though she is only forty-two, she could easily retire and live comfortably off of her investments. Yet she has no thought of retiring. She has an active life outside of work, but her job is something she really enjoys and wants to do, even though she does not need to work from a financial standpoint.

How many of you reading this chapter can say that about your job? If you can, you are one of the small minority, and certainly lucky. Every year, *Fortune* magazine picks the 100 best companies to work for from an employee standpoint. It looks at job security, benefits, compensation, special HR programs, and services like on-site day care and fitness centers. Do you think those things really make people get up in the morning and look forward to coming to work? I don't think so. Sure, we all like good pay, benefits, job security, and special services, but those are not the things that make us love or hate our jobs.

The Gallup company seems to have figured it out. After years of conducting employee satisfaction surveys in various types and sizes of organizations, it has identified twelve questions that really seem to determine whether employees love or hate their jobs. Three themes stand out in the research Gallup has done. They are:

138

1. Having close friends at work (this is vitally important to job satisfaction)
2. Having a job that you are extremely good at and have a passion for
3. Respecting your supervisor or boss

More than anything else, these three factors seem to have the greatest impact on how employees feel about work. What this means is that the window-dressing HR initiatives like employee recognition programs, team-building activities, and other similar initiatives are unlikely to make much difference. Three things an organization can do that do make a difference are:

1. Slot people into jobs for which they have talent and passion.
2. Engineer experiences to build friendships among employees.
3. Carefully screen and select each and every leader, especially first-line supervisors.

These three things sound like common sense and they are inexpensive, yet they are rarely the things that organizations spend time and money on. Instead, they give employees stupid titles like "team members" or "cast members," develop employee-of-the-month programs, give out worthless trinkets and certificates, and expect undying devotion and long hours. Rather than really try to find out what each person's talents are and put them into the best job for their skills, organizations try to develop everyone and move people from job to job without much thought about what they want or the jobs in which they can be most successful. Contrived activities that get billed as "team building" often create more enemies than friends. What builds friendships is experiencing adversity together, such as having to deal with a pain-in-the-butt client or project, or being away from home in a horrible place, or going out for drinks after work and laughing about the customers or your coworkers' antics, or having fun at a company Christmas party. Friendships are rarely created as a result of three-day experiences in the woods in a consultant-led game or exercise.

In order to create a work environment where people love coming to work, you need to spend a lot of effort helping people figure out what they have passion for and what they can be great at. Some of us will never be good managers, writers, speakers, coaches, teachers, engineers, or problem solvers. Many people don't really figure out what they love to do or what they are good at until they are in their forties, and by then they may be to tied into a job or career that they don't like and is too hard to change. When you find people who are very happy in their jobs, you will inevitably find that they have great friends, a great boss, and a job that they sincerely enjoy doing every day.

How to Move It: Do What's Important

❏ ***Don't forget or ignore the importance of employee satisfaction while you're all working toward customer satisfaction.*** Happy employees are productive employees, so you really need to spend some time figuring out what will make your people enjoy coming to work.

❏ ***Do recognize the importance of employee friendships and genuine interest in the work they're doing.*** As much as possible, try to find out what each employee really wants to do and then match that job or assignment with that employee. And give your employees some time—either during the workday, after hours, or at lunch—to truly bond with other people on the staff. Having friends at work is a great way to motivate employees to *want* to come to work every day.

**M
O
V
E
IT**

GET IT

SET IT

MOVE IT

PROVE IT

Review What's Important

There is always a lag between actions and results, but the test of any organization's strategies is whether or not they produce desired results. Investors who bought Internet stocks during 2000 and 2001 were mostly out of luck when their value plummeted a few months later. The value of these companies was not based on sales, profits, or history. Rather, it was based on what looked like great ideas, solid strategies, and plenty of investment capital. The investment capital was quickly burned up, and most of these companies with the letter *e* in their names are gone today. A few Internet companies have survived and prospered, but very few investors have even gotten rich off of investments in these companies.

Proving it is about performance. It is about showing that the things you did in the other chapters of the book really worked. You can follow every piece of advice in this and many other management books and still run into trouble. The key is to develop those early warning signals that tell you a strategy, program, or initiative is not working as you expected. Organizations run on numbers. Even government and nonprofit organizations keep reams of statistics on various things.

The problem with all of these numbers that organizations look at each day and month is that many of the trends and levels of performance are good, but the measures themselves are flawed, so they provide an unrealistic view of performance. An auto company found that the vast majority of customers really liked or loved their cars, but only 40 percent bought another one. The surveys failed to correlate with buying behavior. Most measures of performance are rearview mirror, or based on the past. Many organizations ask themselves questions like:

- How many milestones did we miss last month?
- What were our sales last month?
- How much did we go over budget?

- How many lost-time accidents were there?
- How many employees quit?

All these numbers are good measures of the performance of an organization, but they are all measures of things that have *already* happened and therefore cannot be corrected. *Proving it* is not just about looking at the past to see if your actions worked. *Proving it* is about coming up with leading indicators that predict your future success or failure.

This section of the book is not about accounting principles; there are plenty of good books on that topic. It is about making sure that the numbers you look at to evaluate your business really tell you what you need to know. I talked quite a bit in Part II, the *Set It* section of the book, about coming up with good performance metrics. This final section is about collecting, reporting, and interpreting performance data and using it to analyze performance problems. Looking at flawed numbers has caused many organizations to get into deep hot water before realizing there was a problem. Analyzing trends in data is the easy part. Ensuring the *integrity* of the numbers themselves is much more of a challenge.

Organizations that achieve peak performance and impressive results do the following:

- Require that every program, strategy, and action produces results.
- Ensure the integrity of data with proper checks and balances.
- Report data using consistent formats and easy-to-read graphics.
- Minimize long boring meetings spent reviewing charts and graphs.
- Provide access to real-time data to all employees.
- Link together all databases in a single scorecard that allows for analysis.
- Test theories, hypotheses, and hunches by examining data.
- Look for links between various measures of performance.
- Develop idiot lights or early warning metrics that warn of future problems.

- Analyze the root causes of performance problems by drilling down into the data.
- Realize that numbers are not everything, and that results can include softer measures.

A big part of *proving it* is having the hard evidence in numerical form, which proves the success of your strategies. Not only must you prove it to yourself, you must prove it to shareholders, customers, suppliers, regulators, and others. Anecdotes, feelings, and observations are all important data but not enough to prove success. As the old saying might go: "In God we trust; all others bring data."

Results Take Time

You've heard that line from everybody who has sold you some new software, hardware, or management program. By the time you realize you have been sold a bill of goods, the salespeople and consultants are long gone, working with another organization. The reality is that *results actually do take time*. So patience is a virtue to a point, but if you have to wait too long for something to work, it's too late.

A big financial services firm I worked with spent millions of dollars on a software and consulting firm to help it redesign all its key customer transaction processes, and then customize software to improve the efficiency of the operation. The benefits of this $20+ million expenditure were going to be lower operating costs, higher productivity, happier customers, and happier employees.

Two years into the project, everyone involved was hating life. Employees were totally stressed out by the endless meetings, changes to processes, and trial software products that did not work right. Customers had yet to see any improvements in performance, and in a number of cases, performance had gotten worse. Senior management watched profits shrink as it wrote huge checks to the consultants each month, with continued promises that things would get better and that "results take time."

Eventually, performance in the company did actually improve in some areas but in others the gains in productivity and cost savings never materialized. Improving outcome performance often takes several years, but managers cannot be expected to keep writing checks and just pray that the promised results actually materialize. As the title of a good book suggests: "Hope is not a strategy."

In anything you do, you need to have some data to prove it is working before waiting a year or more. Imagine starting a diet or

PROVE IT

workout program and being told that you won't notice any improvements in your appearance, weight, or energy level for a year or two, but you need to stick with the program. The only thing that keeps anyone focused on any long-term improvement initiative is seeing some early wins or results. The sixteen-year-old who sees his bench press go up by ten pounds in two weeks is very encouraged to keep working out. The dieter who loses two pounds the first week is motivated to stay on the diet.

Organizations need similar data that tell them whether or not a program or strategy is working. Many track what are supposed to be these early successes, but they are false indicators. A client heavily into six sigma for the last two years measures how many employees have been trained as "green belts, brown belts, black belts," and so forth. More and more money was spent each year to train all these experts, yet none of the major measures of company performance had improved. "Be patient, results take time" is what they were told by the six-sigma experts.

Another client has a similar initiative it calls lean sigma, which is a combination of six sigma and lean manufacturing concepts. Rather than track its progress by counting the number of people trained or the number on teams, it measured the performance improvement benefits of a few pilot lean-sigma projects. Things like dollars saved, or cycle time reduced, or other real measures of performance that management cared about were used to assess the effectiveness of the program. Results of these pilot projects actually showed that the lean-sigma effort was working. This is a much more sensible approach than counting teams, or butts in chairs for training.

P
R
O
V
E

I
T

How to Prove It: Review What's Important

❑ *Don't wait too long to see results of improvement programs.* The promoters of many of these programs encourage patience, but keep this in perspective. Major improvements in an organization's overall performance often require a period of several years to materialize. But that doesn't mean you can't evaluate your progress along the way.

❑ *Do keep track of early wins, or early warning signs, that an approach or strategy is not working as you anticipated.* Smart organizations figure out how to do this. When you track these progress measures or small wins, you can then feel comfortable waiting for the big wins to materialize.

P
R
O
V
E

I
T

Develop a Standard Reporting Format

A common reason that organizations fail to detect performance problems is that the methods used to report and communicate data are poorly designed. The most common format for reports is spreadsheets with many columns of numbers printed in tiny type fonts. Executives with aging eyes squint while trying to see the numbers to determine if performance is above or below the target, and there are so many numbers on each sheet, it's little wonder that things get missed. What exacerbates the problem even further is that there is page after page of data like this in a typical monthly management report.

Along with these spreadsheet reports, executives and managers must usually attend a monthly meeting in which hundreds of Power-Point charts are reviewed. Many days and long hours are spent each month preparing for these meetings and each presenter often has fifteen to twenty-five charts showing performance in his or her area. Some presenters like bar charts, others like pie charts, scatter diagrams, line graphs, or other more complicated displays of data, often with many different trends on one chart of intersecting lines. Half the time in these meetings is spent trying to decipher the charts themselves to determine if performance is good or bad.

Northrop Grumman and a number of other clients with whom I've worked have established a standardized format for presenting performance data in any meeting or report. When looking at any measure of performance, you need to know three things:

1. Level: What is the current level of performance compared to your target?

2. Trend: How does performance look over time—better, worse, or flat, and how much variability in performance is there?
3. Explanation: What happened to make performance get better, worse, or stay the same?

Several clients require a fourth field of information to be filled in called the *action plan*, wherein they must explain what is being done to improve poor performance or stop a declining trend.

Many organizations avoid the monthly preparation of charts and graphs by using scorecard software to display live performance data in meetings. Data is displayed in color-coded gauges and charts, and analyses can be done live in the meeting to determine the root cause of problems. The gauges usually represent the overall performance in that specific area. The warning lights, however, act as an indicator that there might be a specific problem because they point out the lower end of the measure's average. In addition, warning lights may prompt a closer look at the specifics of the data.

There is no single right way to communicate performance data, but whatever format you decide on, stay consistent. Some general rules to follow are to:

- Use colors (e.g., red, yellow, green) to depict performance versus targets.
- Display both current performance and trends over time.
- Avoid showing unnecessary backup data supporting each overall metric.
- Apply the six-foot rule for all presentation slides—you should be able to read the chart from six feet away.
- Use commercial scorecard software to avoid preparing charts every month and allow for real-time data analysis.

P
R
O
V
E

I
T

How to Prove It: Review What's Important

❏ *Don't waste time creating overly detailed, unreadable status reports and spreadsheets.* And don't waste time holding frequent meetings to discuss these. Remember, your employees can actually *do* the work you hired them to do, or they can spend their time *reporting* on the work they're supposed to be doing. Keep your priorities straight, and your employees will be more productive.

❏ *Do set up a simple, easy-to-read and easy-to-update system to track performance.* Many organizations use scorecard software to facilitate this; the important criterion is that the system you use should be simple.

P
R
O
V
E

I
T

Put Idiot Lights on
Your Dashboard

It's always a major challenge for me to convince executives with engineering or technical backgrounds that they don't need to look at seventy-five or more charts every month to assess company performance. Engineers, accountants, and others with a more analytical nature love looking at numbers, and the more they look at, the more comfortable they are with company performance. After all, most have been trained to analyze and trust data, which is the foundation of most scientific disciplines.

An approach that I have found works well for executives is to make most of their performance gauges indices that are made up of four to six submeasures. Each of those Tier-2 measures are made up of four to six Tier-3 metrics, and so forth. An index gives you an overall view of performance, as the Dow Jones or Standard & Poor's index does of overall market performance. Most investors are content checking the Dow or NASDAQ indices each day, rather than looking up the performance of each of the companies in which they own stock. Executives need to adopt the same mentality when it comes to the performance indices on their dashboards.

Organizations I've worked with have constructed indices relating to customer loyalty, employee satisfaction, intellectual capital, revenue growth, and a variety of other factors. Each index should focus on a singular dimension of performance. The good thing about an index is that it can give you a good overview of performance without making you look at many different charts. The bad thing about an index is that it can hide important changes in

P
R
O
V
E

I
T

performance that a manager or executive should be paying attention to. For example, one submeasure gets better, another gets worse; they cancel each other out, and the index gauge does not move—it stays in the "green zone."

For an index to work, you also need to have an idiot or warning light attached to each gauge. The warning light turns only red or yellow, and it alerts the manger to look under the hood by drilling down into the data to find out what is causing the idiot light to turn on.

The manager keeps drilling down by business unit, location, and department, and finds that the cause of the warning light is the contracts department in the Denver office, which is part of the government business unit. Further analysis on this data might reveal that there is extremely high turnover, and the notes indicate that a major competitor has successfully recruited away a large number of your contracts people.

The warning lights on the dashboard allow detailed-oriented analytical managers to be comfortable with indices or gauges that provide a summary of performance, as long as the idiot light tells them when to look under the hood and delve deeper into the data. If the overall index is green and the warning light is not on, there is no need to go into more detailed data. This approach can save countless hours in meetings looking at detailed charts that don't need to be looked at. One client that adopted this approach cut its monthly executive review meetings down from eight hours to two hours because it only goes into detail on the indices that are red or yellow, or those that have the warning light turned on.

Most commercial scorecard software has this idiot light feature, and most programs allow individual managers to set the limits for turning on the warning lights. One manager might set it at a very low threshold, causing the light to go on if there is a slight problem in even a tiny part of an organization. Another manager might decide to set it at a very high threshold, expecting all the people that report to her to manage the lower levels of performance.

How to Prove It: Review What's Important

❏ ***Don't get bogged down in too much data or too many reports.*** Many organizations, especially with lots of technical people, tend to do this because they're most comfortable reviewing lots of data. But you need to pay most attention to performance problems, so you need some type of system that alerts you to these, rather than reviewing everything constantly.

❏ ***Do set up a "warning light" system.*** Think of this as similar to the warning light on the dashboard of a car, only your system should call attention to specific problem areas that are appropriate for the type of work you're doing. Fortunately, most commercial scorecard software offers this feature.

P
R
O
V
E

I
T

Ensure the Integrity of Your Data

Once you start tracking performance on a metric and holding people accountable for results, you have set up a reason for them to cheat. I mentioned back in Chapter 43 that you need to balance trust and control, but it is best not to have the fox guarding the henhouse. A national real estate company I worked with relied heavily on customer satisfaction feedback from home buyers and sellers. Agents were told to hand out surveys at the end of each customer transaction and encourage the customers to send them back. From what I recall, they did get a fairly high return rate of over 60 percent. The agents were selective about who they handed them out to, however. They knew when a customer was not real happy with their performance, so they never even mentioned the survey to those customers. The ones they knew were delighted with the agent and the transaction got a survey and lots of encouragement to fill it out. By relying on the agents to distribute the surveys themselves the system lacked integrity, and the data did not reflect reality.

One good way of ensuring integrity in your data is to use an outside firm to gather the data. As in an employee morale survey, this helps ensure anonymity for the responders and prevents managers and employees from stacking the deck in their favor. Many industries besides the automotive industry now use J. D. Power to conduct their customer satisfaction surveys. One of the major car companies with whom I worked told me that they caught many of their dealerships cheating on the J. D. Power surveys. Service advisors would call up consumers a few weeks before the survey went out, suggesting that if the customer gave excellent ratings to the dealership and brought in a photocopy after sending the original to J. D. Power, the dealership would detail their car for free during the next service appointment.

It turned out that this practice was not limited to this car company, dealers of most car brands were doing this. There are negative consequences to getting poor customer satisfaction scores, so the crafty dealers have figured out how to get good scores without really improving service—they use bribery. In spite of this, it is still better to use an outside firm to gather data where possible.

Another approach to ensuring integrity in your data is to minimize the number of metrics that are based on judgment and try to count things like dollars in sales or lost accounts. The challenge is that many of the metrics based on counting involve counting stupid things like butts in chairs in training, number of customers visited, Web site hits, and so forth. Many of the most important things to measure about organizational performance cannot be measured simply by counting—there must be some judgment involved. Where you need to use judgment metrics, you can improve the integrity of the data through descriptive measurement scales, rater training, and periodic audits or reliability checks to ensure interrater consistency.

As a general rule, you do not want to have a group measure its own performance, especially if it is held accountable for the results on that metric. This is why we have departments such as auditing, quality control, finance, and "inspector general" groups in the government and military. Having one group measure the performance of another one tends to add more objectivity to the data, but this approach is not without flaws, either. Sometimes the two groups will work together to make each other look good, although this is quite rare, as there are often serious consequences to such actions.

It is important to run an organization by looking at performance numbers, so those numbers must be valid and honest reflections of real performance. In order to ensure the integrity of your performance data be sure to:

- Use objective metrics based on counting whenever possible.

P
R
O
V
E

I
T

- Ensure consistency in judgment metrics by using descriptive scales, training raters, and performing periodic reliability checks.
- Use outside organizations to measure performance whenever possible.
- Check for inconsistencies in related measures to identify possible problems.
- Conduct periodic audits of performance data to uncover data integrity problems.
- Communicate the importance of honest reporting to employees and deal severely with those caught cheating on performance measures.

How to Prove It: Review What's Important

❏ *Don't let your employees track their own performance.* This just isn't the best way to measure how well you're doing, because there's not enough control built into this approach. Also, don't assume that an outside organization or another department is automatically objective, because there are ways to beat, or cheat, any system.

❏ *Do establish auditing or inspecting departments to measure performance periodically.* This is the best way to ensure the integrity of your performance data.

P
R
O
V
E

I
T

Forget "Statistically Significant"

The concept of statistically significant is important to science, so it can rule out the likelihood that differences between the experimental and control group are due to the independent variable and not chance. The difference between statistically significant and chance results are often slight, but great enough to be statistically significant to science. Most businesses and government organizations are not concerned with doing research and proving things. Rather, they are concerned with good performance. A program, strategy, or action might have a statistically significant impact on performance but fail to produce a practical impact.

A recent example from a major discount department store chain comes to mind. This company wanted to find the correlations between employee morale, customer satisfaction, and revenue. Other research suggests that there are tight links between happy employees, happy customers, and happy shareholders. Southwest Airlines, known to have some of the happiest employees in the airline industry, certainly has many happy customers, and shareholders as well, as the company has shown a profit in many years while its competitors have shown losses.

The discount chain found that it needed a 5 percent improvement in employee morale to achieve a 1 percent improvement in customer satisfaction to get one-half of 1 percent improvement in sales revenue. For each dollar in sales revenue, a retailer like this one usually earns a few cents in profit. Achieving a 5 percent improvement in employee satisfaction would probably require some major expen-

P
R
O
V
E
I
T

ditures and efforts that are unlikely to pay off on the bottom line. The links between these three measures might be *statistically* significant, but certainly not *practically* significant. These numbers suggest that it would be hard to get a good return on investment by improving either employee morale or customer satisfaction. To get even a 1 percent improvement in sales would require a 10 percent improvement in employee morale.

When examining results in your organization, it is important to determine whether your efforts are actually working to drive improvement in outcomes. For example, a government regulatory agency might find that a 10 percent increase in audit frequency results in a 20 percent reduction in cheating or a similar improvement in compliance measures. It is important to try things out like this to see if you can get enough improvement to recover the resources needed for the new program or effort. The government agency would need to do a cost–benefit analysis on the resources required for the additional auditing to see if the improved results are worth the effort. The Internal Revenue Service certainly applies this principal in deciding who is most likely to receive an audit.

When you are evaluating various strategies, programs, and activities it is vitally important to show that they produce results, as I suggest in Chapter 53. It is even more important to show that the improvements noted are worth the cost. The U.S. government spends millions of dollars each year to try to reduce drug use. The lion's share of that money goes toward an advertising campaign called "Say No to Drugs." This campaign certainly uses a lot of tax dollars for TV commercials, print ads, billboards, radio spots, and school programs. All these things make the politicians look good and make us feel good but, in my opinion, they don't work. In spite of millions of dollars we spend on advertising, drug use continues to increase. Even if drug use had declined by a few percentage points, it would probably not be enough to warrant the continued expenditures for the advertising campaign.

PROVE IT

How to Prove It: Review What's Important

❏ *Don't apply the concept of statistical significance when evaluating the results of any improvement effort in your organization.* Statistical significance is for scientists, not business managers. It's just not helpful in tracking work performance.

❏ *Do concentrate on those initiatives that produce a practical return for the resources you invest.* You can't spend your time measuring everything, so measure what is important.

P
R
O
V
E

I
T

Look for Links Between Hard and Soft Metrics

A big utility in the Midwest has been tracking measures of employee morale, customer satisfaction, diversity, employee education, and various other "softer" measures on its corporate scorecard for years. It does look at performance on these softer metrics in a monthly one-hour meeting, but it has another meeting once a month where financial and operational results are reviewed, that lasts most of the day. Further, the bonuses that executives receive are tied only to the financial measures. A $2 billion chemical company in Pennsylvania had a balanced set of measures as well. Back when I worked with it, 95 percent of the executive bonuses was for financial performance; 5 percent was for performance on all the other gauges. What this says is that the company had no faith in the nonfinancial metrics.

This is actually fairly typical, and these two companies are among the majority that do not really believe that results on the softer measures really link to the hard measures of profits, growth, and increase in share price. Consequently, they are unwilling to pay for these things. Also, you can cheat on these other measures, whereas everyone knows you can't cheat on financial results, right? Right—just ask WorldCom and Enron.

The problem with this approach is that almost all financial metrics are measures of the past, as are outcome metrics for government organizations. Executives often believe there is a link between employee morale, customer satisfaction, and outcomes, but they are not sure how strong the link is, and they do not trust the data as much as the financials.

In order to convince executives that the softer measures really do matter, and that these results can lead to improvements in outcomes and finances, you need to *prove it*. So how do you prove this? With data. A financial services firm I worked with found that if it made enough small mistakes on customer accounts, or made a couple of big mistakes, customers would leave, never to return. In fact, it found the reverse to be true as well. By reducing errors it could increase customer loyalty and drive up profits, because long-term loyal customers are more profitable than new ones that have to be lured with expensive marketing campaigns. What this company also found was that you reach the point of diminishing returns when it comes to reducing errors. Customers would forgive them for an occasional minor mistake, and the effort required to get to zero defects would not drive enough increased customer loyalty to pay off. As a result of this data on the links between operational errors, customer loyalty, and profits, senior management paid much more attention to the data on operational quality than in the past.

Sometimes these links between measures are discovered by accident, rather than through a planned experiment. A pharmaceutical firm found that a decrease in visit frequency by their sales reps actually improved customer satisfaction, when it expected satisfaction to decline. It had to increase the territory of sales reps so they had to visit doctors less often, and focus groups later revealed that doctors thought more favorably about the company because a sales rep was not always in their office bugging them when they had work to do.

If you ever hope to get senior management to pay attention to your softer measures, such as corporate culture, employee satisfaction, intellectual capital, and customer loyalty, you need to prove to them that these metrics link to things they care about. Executives in government care about outcomes, and image or public opinion. Executives in business care about growth, profits, and share price. If you can prove that there are practically significant links between your softer measures and these outcomes, you can bet they will start paying attention to them, and possibly even linking pay to them, like Ford, FedEx, and other forward-thinking companies.

P
R
O
V
E

I
T

How to Prove It: Review What's Important

❑ *Don't just give lip service to tracking changes in "soft" measures like employee morale and customer satisfaction.* Companies that do this usually lose both valuable employees and customers, even if their "hard" measures of sales and profits look good for a while.

❑ *Do try to find the link between your hard and soft measures.* This data and information helps everyone in your organization pay more attention to the soft stuff, instead of just focusing on the financial numbers.

P
R
O
V
E

I
T

Prove the Value of Your Results Measures

Organizations love to count things, prepare reports and presentations, and go to meetings to look at statistics. A client that manufactured police radios liked to count the number of new customers it acquired each month and the number of proposals it had written. The president had a vision to dramatically grow the company in size, and become a thorn in the side of Motorola, which dominated the market. Every month the president held a sales meeting, where the executives looked at the number of new customers and proposals. Whenever the aggressive targets were hit, everyone celebrated and became more motivated to hit the next month's target.

This went on for several years, while account executives were bidding on more jobs and bringing in lots of new customers each month. After a couple of years, the company found itself in big trouble. The salespeople had made all sorts of promises about the company's radios and technology that stretched the truth. When the systems failed to perform as promised or sometimes failed to work at all, the company began to be plagued with lawsuits from angry police departments. Some of the suits came from departments in major cities like Miami and Honolulu, and word about the company and its radios spread among the police community. Pretty soon, its image was so bad that few major police departments would even let them bid on a job, let alone award it to them. Motorola was always the safe choice, and no one ever got fired for buying Motorola radios for its police department.

P
R
O
V
E

I
T

The police radio company also found that although sales had increased dramatically, costs had escalated at a much higher rate, and the business was running in the red. The president was eventually let go, and a new guy was brought in to save the company from the mess it was in. The cause of this company's problems is not too hard to figure out. A growth vision was appropriate since the company had to become a bigger player to compete against Motorola, which owned more than 75 percent of the market.

The problem was that the two measures it focused on, number of new customers and number of proposals, drove the wrong behavior. The president and sales vice president focused on these two measures more than any others, and salespeople were given bonuses for writing proposals and winning new accounts. The flaw in the system was that no one looked at the *quality* of the new accounts they were going after or the *profitability* of the business once it was won. Salespeople would cut prices, promise things that could not be delivered, and do whatever it took to prevent Motorola or another competitor from getting the award. Once the contract was won, it was someone else's problem to make the system perform as promised. By focusing on these two results to the exclusion of others, the company got itself in big trouble.

The new president created a couple of better results measures that ended up driving the right behavior. The first was called "Opportunity Strategic Value Index." It was a measure of the quality of a sales prospect or potential customer. The score included factors such as:

- Dollar value of the sale
- Projected gross margin
- Ease of meeting the customer's requirements
- Name recognition of the customer (Would it impress other police departments?)
- Location (Do we have an office near the customer?)
- Likelihood of award (chances of winning the bid)
- Politics (Are the any political factors in our favor?)

The second measure focused on the quality of the new account once it was won, and included factors similar to those mentioned.

The new measures caused salespeople to be selective about what they bid on, knowing that they would be held accountable for the profitability of the sale, and with the level of the customers' satisfaction once the radio systems were installed.

The lesson here is that you need to make sure that the results you are focusing on really drive the right behavior. Making one gauge green sometimes causes another to turn red, so you need to think hard about what you really want and the price you will pay to achieve it.

How to Prove It: Review What's Important

❏ ***Don't measure the wrong things.*** Many companies think they're doing well because some aspect of its business is up—higher, faster, or better—but this "improvement" doesn't always take into consideration all the other factors, which often include quality and profitability, that contribute to that change. Also, don't ignore all the departments that may be adversely affected because of the changes you're making elsewhere.

❏ ***Do understand all of the ramifications of the improvements you're striving for.*** Make sure the results you're targeting really reinforce the right behavior among all your employees.

P
R
O
V
E

I
T

The Importance of
Comparative Data

A California county government organization I've worked with for many years had a vision of being the "best run county in America." When I asked the county CEO which was currently the best run county in America, or even California for that matter, he had no idea, but he said he wanted to be number one. In order for you to interpret your results, you need to have lots of data on competitors, industry averages, industry bests (benchmarks), comparable organizations. In fact, it is really impossible to evaluate how well you are doing unless you have someone else to compare to. An Air Force client showed me that many of their measures of performance on operational measures in support functions indicated that they were among the best in the Air Force. When asked how the Air Force compared to others who maintained facilities and vehicles, provided medical services, issued purchase orders, and performed other functions, he had no idea. Someone in the meeting where these results were being reviewed suggested that the data might show that the base was the "cream of the crap."

Proving your success and the validity of your results requires gathering data on competitors and other like organizations. I recall working with office furniture maker Haworth, and looking at its results, which were mostly flat over a five-year period. Sales, margins, new customers, and other financial measures showed a flat trend and levels that for the most part did not hit their targets. The results took on an entirely new light when they showed that every one of the three major competitors had experienced significant declines in performance over the same time frame and that the entire office furniture industry had experienced these declines. The fact that Haworth was able to maintain stability in its results was truly impressive in a bad economy.

Getting data on how your industry is performing is easy. Most professional organizations track this sort of thing, as do market analysts and even some government organizations like the U.S. Department of Commerce or the U.S. Department of Labor. There really is no excuse for not having industry data against which to compare your performance. Competitor data is a bit harder to acquire, but most organizations manage to get it somehow. The important data to get describes the performance of the top three or four organizations that are your most direct competition, or for a government organization, the ones that are the most like you. For example, the Veteran's Administration compares its hospitals and clinics to other hospitals and clinics of similar size, specialization, and resource constraints.

It is important to compare your own performance to benchmark or best organizations, along with competitive data, even though the organizations might not be direct competitors. For example, an airline might compare some of their results to FedEx: They are both in the business of moving stuff from one place to another. An Internet service provider might compare its call center performance to that of a phone company or bank.

The reason for all this comparative data is to be able to realistically assess your own results. Hitting your own internally set targets is not very meaningful, since many of these targets are set arbitrarily and are strictly based on your past performance. It really is impossible to evaluate your own levels and trends in performance without quite a bit of competitive data. Your gauge could all show green levels of performance and upward trends, and your guys are walking around high-fiving each other, when in reality you should be very concerned. A competitor might be rapidly gaining on you or consistently outperforming you because you set your targets too low.

P
R
O
V
E

I
T

How to Prove It: Review What's Important

Proving it means proving to others outside of your organization that you are good, not just proving it to your self. You need to prove your performance to shareholders, customers, taxpayers, Congress, and many others, and you need comparative data to do that. Here's how to *prove it*:

❏ ***Don't track only your own performance and compare it to previous years.*** This is valuable information to have, but the key word is *only*: you need to do more than this or you're operating your business in a vacuum, with no idea how the rest of the world—which includes your competition—is doing. And without that competitive information, you could lose your customers and your entire business any day.

❏***Do monitor at least three or four of your key competitors and compare your own performance to theirs.*** General industry information is easy to find, and with some effort you should also be able to get some information on your primary competitors. This comparative data is critical for benchmarking, and for making sure that you stay ahead of—or at least keep up with—the rest of the pack.

P
R
O
V
E

I
T

Every Program, Initiative, and Strategy Needs to Produce Results

I've facilitated a lot of strategic planning meetings where strategies and projects for achieving goals are identified. One of my clients had a goal that focused on improving communication with customers, employees, and contractors. It came up with a long list of strategies to improve communication and narrowed down the list to a few key things:

- Communication skills training for everyone
- A new communication policy
- A monthly newsletter and weekly e-mail news release for employees and others
- New project management software that included communication mechanisms

Several hundred thousands of dollars were spent on the projects listed. The next year, the planning retreat was held in a different location, and the team that owned the communication goal reported that communication had improved and that the goal had been achieved. Highlights of its presentation included the following:

- The new communication policy was written in February, released in March, and distributed to all relevant employees.
- Eighty-two percent of the employees and many contractors had attended the communication training.
- The new software was purchased in May and was being used on about one-third of the existing projects, and all new ones.

**P
R
O
V
E

I
T**

- Newsletters were being written and distributed on a regular basis.

The big problem that no one wanted to bring up was that none of this data indicated that communication was any better. There had been a lot of money spent, and a lot of activity, and lots of information was disseminated, but had communication improved? No one really knew it had, but no one in the meeting had any data to the contrary.

Many large organizations go through the experience of having a planning meeting, developing goals, formulating strategies, taking action, and then not knowing whether or not its strategies worked. There are a lot of politics in these planning meetings, and only the most foolhardy person would question the effectiveness of one of the executives' pet projects.

Another client in the credit card business set a goal of getting two million new cardholding customers. The strategies involved direct mail, advertising, and telemarketing. The next year it reported that the goal of acquiring two million new card-carrying customers had been achieved. It had also succeeded in getting balance transfers of hundreds of millions of dollars. The problem that no one in the planning meeting wanted to talk about was the quality of the balance transfers and the credit worthiness of the new customers. The company had slightly lowered its standards in order to attract more new customers and ended up with a lot of bad debt and a lot of high-risk customers, which ultimately put a big dent in profits the following year.

Was the growth strategy a success? No. A business does not want more bad customers on whom it cannot make a profit. For every strategy, initiative, project, action plan, or new campaign you develop, you need to be able to *prove* its success. *Proving it* means being able to demonstrate the value of some effort or activity. It means more than just showing that you spent money and did a lot of things. *Proving it* means showing a clear cause and effect between your strategies and some bottom-line results.

P R O V E I T

How to Prove It: Review What's Important

❑ *Don't embark on any new initiative, strategy, or program without first identifying the measures that will be used to prove the effectiveness of the effort.* Define exactly what success will look like.

❑ *Do make sure that the changes you implement affect the bottom line.* New or revised policies, strategies, and plans should improve some tangible measurement, whether it's productivity, profitability, or customer service—which leads to increased customer retention.

P
R
O
V
E

I
T

Show Me the Money

Fifteen years ago, a popular measure of performance was called the price of nonconformance, or PONC. Many organizations began to track how much money they waste fixing things that weren't done right the first time, and most found that millions were being spent on poor quality. I recall working with a major high-end European auto manufacturer that told me that about 30 percent of the cost of its cars was on rework. After being alarmed at this staggering statistic, many organizations began forming teams to study work processes, analyze the causes of waste and errors, and reduce the dollars spent on poor quality.

A few pilot projects showed that ten to one returns on time invested were not uncommon. Teams redesigned processes, improved inspections, and every employee in the organization attended a long and expensive series of workshops on analyzing and improving quality. Reports were prepared that showed that hundreds of millions of dollars were often being saved. Sure, the training was expensive, and there was the big opportunity cost of having all these people attend team meetings when they could be working, but the cost savings were huge, so the effort continued. Not only was this occurring in the business world, but government and military organizations were heavily invested in reducing the price of PONC as well.

There were a few executives who remained skeptical, but even they were impressed by the graphs showing major cost savings. The problem with all these dollars in cost savings earned is that they never seemed to end up in anyone's budget or bank account. No one got rid of any people, so there were no real labor cost savings. Budgets were not reduced at all and often continued to increase. Even reduced manufacturing costs or service delivery costs rarely seemed to add more profit to the bottom line. So where were all those millions of dollars in savings? First of all, in many cases, this was not real money—rather, it was hypothetical cost savings. Second, people fudged the statistics on rework time and costs to make the numbers look better. Finally, the real money that was saved was spent on other things like computers, people, supplies, and equipment. Most of the dollars that were saved from quality improvement initiatives did not improve profitability or efficiency.

Fast-forward to the present day, and a very similar phenomenon is happening. Today, we don't talk about the price of nonconformance. Today, we talk about customer relationship management, activity-based costing, balanced scorecard, integrated product development, six sigma, and lean manufacturing. These analytical approaches for defining opportunities for improvement and changing work processes to improve performance look suspiciously like the TQM programs of the past. Of course, these performance improvement initiatives are not just about improving quality. They are methodologies that have often been used to reduce costs, cycle times, and waste; and improve efficiency. Organizations are now training "green belts," "black belts," and expert internal consultants to guide teams in analyzing and improving performance.

Guess how these organizations today are measuring the impact of these "new" programs? The most popular measure is dollars in cost savings attributed to improvement projects. And guess how many of those dollars in cost savings wind up in someone's real bank account or budget? You guessed it—very few. These hypothetical cost savings are a very dangerous way to measure the success of any program. I don't mean to downgrade the effectiveness of six sigma, lean, or other similar initiatives, because I have seen a number of organizations generate substantial real improvements in costs and other factors. These approaches really do work. What I am suggesting is that proving the effectiveness of these programs involves a lot more than tracking hypothetical cost savings.

P
R
O
V
E

I
T

How to Prove It: Review What's Important

Proving it means "show me the money." Next time you are in a meeting where they are reviewing the success of the latest process improvement projects, challenge the presenters to show you how and where the real cost savings come from. Ask questions like: "When can we expect to reduce your budget due to the cost savings from this project?" A few leading organizations actually do this, and require a reduction in resources commensurate with the cost savings from process improvement projects. Most do not, however. Here's how to *prove it*:

❑ ***Don't judge the success or failure of your improvement initiatives on the basis of projected or hypothetical results.*** You can't spend or invest anticipated cost savings; you need real tangible results.

❑ ***Do challenge all projected cost savings by asking for details on how, when, and from where the money will be realized.*** This is the only way to really reduce costs.

Let the Data Tell You When to Change

Organizations often keep doing the same things over and over again, when you'd think there would be enough evidence that those strategies or actions are not producing results. On the other hand, I've seen organizations kill successful programs, initiatives, and strategies when they are clearly working. Often a new boss will change programs or strategies just because they were associated with the previous boss or administration. The Malcolm Baldrige model had been used for years by federal government organizations to structure their improvement efforts. Millions of dollars had been saved by the president's Quality Award–winning government organizations, and the program cost only a few hundred thousand dollars to administer. When George W. Bush took office, one of his initial actions was to cancel the president's Quality Award. He backpedaled a little later when he was told that his father helped create the award, but he stuck to his guns, and months later unveiled a new award based on his own President's Management Agenda. The decision to cancel the award was not based on data—the data showed that the award program was a resounding success. The decision was politically motivated.

Organizations that are really results oriented let the data tell them when and how to change their approaches. A new boss would be crazy to change things that are clearly working, even if they might be associated with the previous administration. Yet bosses do crazy things, and most new bosses want to show people that they have a new and different approach, so they sometimes change things that they shouldn't change.

One of the keys to being a results-oriented organization is to measure results often enough to be able to tell that something is working. A client implemented a number of changes and new programs to improve employee morale. Anecdotal data indicated that employees were happy with the efforts, and HR was getting lots of positive comments from management. However, the client had to wait for almost a year to find out that its efforts did not improve employee satisfaction at all. It measured morale via an annual survey, so it had no other way to measure the impact of its efforts. By the time an entire year had passed, many resources were wasted in efforts that did nothing to improve morale.

Another client did a similar thing with customer satisfaction. An expensive software-driven process called customer relationship management (CRM) was implemented to improve the satisfaction and loyalty levels of customers. Again, the measure was an annual survey of customers. This client learned too late that the expensive and time-consuming CRM system did not really affect customers' opinions or loyalty. As a general rule, annual metrics on anything are close to worthless. The problem is that you have to wait twelve months to get another data point, and a lot of money and other valuable resources could be wasted over the course of a year.

Leading organizations collect monthly or at least quarterly statistics on all important aspects of their performance. The more frequently you can measure results, the better. The other side of this, which you need to consider, is the cost and practicality of more-frequent performance measurement. If you are stuck doing employee or customer surveys, do them more frequently with a sample of people. For example, one client surveys one-twelfth of the employee population each month so it gets a monthly data point on morale, but no one fills out the survey more than once a year.

After you have begun tracking more frequent measures, you can then study the trends in your weekly or monthly results measures to evaluate the impact of any strategies, programs, or initiatives. Something to be careful of is canceling a program or effort before it has had a chance to work. Many things do take time to produce results, but remember my warnings from Chapter 45, about being

PROVE IT

too patient. Often a strategy will work like gangbusters for a year or two, and then results will start to plateau. Studying the data will tell you this as well. Don't expect to get dramatic improvements that you might have experienced at first. A stable trend might not be a bad thing, as long as levels of performance are excellent.

How to Prove It: Review What's Important

❏ ***Don't change what works, and don't keep doing things that don't work.*** Often, a new boss will do this just to make his or her mark on the organization, but this isn't a good way to improve performance. Also, don't review only once a year: That's too infrequent and therefore too long to wait to see if performance is truly improving.

❏ ***Do use the results data to determine your next steps.*** Measure whatever you're tracking on a monthly or at least a quarterly basis so you don't waste too much time evaluating the impact of any given strategy or plan. A shorter measurement cycle makes you more nimble and able to react more swiftly.

**P
R
O
V
E

I
T**

Streamline the Dreaded Monthly Review Meeting

Every month, thousands of organizations, large and small, get their top managers and executives together for the dreaded monthly review meeting. Much preparation goes into these meetings, with armies of clerks working overtime to prepare hundreds of Power-Point charts and spreadsheets for presentation. Changes are often inserted at the last minute, so there are often multiple drafts of each slide prepared. The meeting begins with the boss providing an update on company news or highlighting some of the major successes of the month: "Let's give Audrey and her team a big round of applause for landing the Sanderson deal after a year and a half of hard work."

Following the congratulations and news briefs, we begin the process of reviewing the performance of each unit in the organization, one by one. Each executive gets up for thirty to sixty minutes to present his or her slides. The executives all jockey for position on the agenda. Being among the first few to present is the worst time slot because everyone is wide awake and much more likely to challenge and analyze your performance in excruciating detail. Most of the questions relate to understanding your charts and challenging your results, rather than analyzing the causes of poor performance. By the time 3 P.M. rolls around, everyone is pretty much brain dead from watching several hundred slides, so they are more likely to just let you review your slides quickly without questions or challenges. By then, most people just want the meeting to be over and are having trouble staying awake through the endless litany of boring presentations and slides that are unreadable and often undecipherable.

P
R
O
V
E

I
T

There is a better way. These monthly meetings are an incredible waste of time and money in many business and government organizations. The most highly paid people in the organization are tied up for an entire day, looking at charts. Several clients have adopted a better approach to reviewing performance. First of all, all performance data resides in a central database that can be accessed by the managers at any time and from any location. Many companies have a private Web site for their performance data. Results are usually updated on a daily or even hourly basis for a number of the metrics, so managers are looking at real-time data, not ancient history. Performance is presented in color-coded gauges and trend charts, so it is easy to scan the company scorecard to look for problem areas. Idiot lights or red–yellow gauges alert mangers to drill down further into the data, but such analysis is unnecessary when performance levels and trends are positive. Managers are expected to review the performance of their units on a regular basis from their desks, rather than wait for a monthly review. The purpose of the new monthly meeting is not to look at performance results. Rather, its purpose is to analyze areas of problem performance and develop strategies for improving it.

What used to be an eight- to ten-hour monthly meeting for one of my military clients is now a two- to three-hour meeting. One of the major cost savings improvements is that no longer do any charts need to be prepared. The command's scorecard database is hooked up to an LCD projector so that live data can be presented and analyzed. The only data presented in the meeting are those graphs and gauges showing red or yellow performance or downward trends. There is no need to present good performance in a meeting. The boss begins with a summary of some of the best results for the month so that performers still get some kudos for their good work, but this only requires about fifteen minutes.

The major focus of the meeting is analyzing the causes of subpar performance and using the expertise of the group to develop action plans or improvement strategies. This approach not only saves the leaders valuable time, the meeting itself is infinitely more productive and interesting. No one dozes off like they used to.

P
R
O
V
E

I
T

Attendees are actively involved in helping to figure out how to improve results, rather than just looking at them.

How to Prove It: Review What's Important

❑ ***Don't waste valuable employees' time preparing slide shows for internal meetings.*** Detailed reviews of how they're performing are unnecessary; worse, they detract from your employees' time doing real work.

❑ ***Do create a database to capture real-time performance data.*** Of course, all organizations need to track how well they're doing. But there are so many easier, more effective and efficient ways to do this that can—and should—replace a daylong meeting.

The Emperor's New Clothes

Remember the old story about the emperor's new clothes, in which his disciples refused to let him know he was naked because he was so pleased with what he thought was a new and beautiful set of clothes? It's kind of a stupid story, but you have no doubt observed this sort of thing happening in your own organization many times. The bosses are so enamored with a new strategy, program, acquisition, or project that no one wants to tell them that they are not working. The organization continues to invest money, time, and other valuable resources in approaches that do nothing to improve performance. The emperor is clearly naked, but no one wants to tell him.

The most common program I've seen many large organizations waste a lot of money on is leadership development training. In twenty-five years of consulting with large organizations, I've seen a lot of similarity in these programs. The typical program is three days in length and begins with some pop psychology assessment instrument like Myers-Briggs or a knockoff version. Attendees complete the questionnaire and learn to put themselves in one of the boxes on the instrument used to classify people's personalities. Participants share their ratings with peers and discuss the differences in their personal styles with the facilitator. This exercise often takes about half a day, it is fun, and rarely are there any surprises. The people that everyone knows are more intuitive or analytical end up being categorized this way by the instrument.

After finding out how to classify your personality, there is usually a presentation on a recent management book that happens to be in vogue. Following this there are usually a series of modules on topics such as negotiating, planning, coaching, mentoring, resolving conflicts, strategic thinking, problem solving, and so forth. Rarely is

P
R
O
V
E

I
T

more than an hour or two spent on each topic, so there are no skills developed, and even the level of knowledge communicated is superficial. On the second day, there is often a team-building exercise that may extend into the evening. On the third day, there is almost always a case study that must be completed by teams. Teams report their analysis of the case study at the end of the day, and everyone heads home or off to the airport.

The challenge with any of these leadership development programs is *proving* that they really help make better leaders and managers. I have never heard a successful CEO or executive claim that her success was due to a great three-day course she attended that taught her how to be a great leader. Some of the best leaders I've met don't bother attending such programs because they have better things to do. Other managers have attended more than a dozen leadership development programs, and they remain barely competent as leaders. Many skills of being a good manager can be taught, but they are not often taught in these three-day programs.

A few companies, such as GE, are known to have outstanding leadership development programs. GE really does seem to be good at grooming competent leaders. Most organizations do not have programs like GE's and really have no idea whether or not their leadership programs work. The measures of success are how many people attended the programs (butts in chairs) and the feedback questionnaires filled out by attendees at the end of the course. If the instructor was entertaining, the content was interesting, and the exercises were fun, the course will undoubtedly get good marks from the attendees. The purpose of these programs is to groom more effective leaders, however, not to entertain them.

Proving the effectiveness of leadership development or similar programs involves a little effort and creativity. One company I worked with tried to show a correlation between attendance in leadership development programs and the speed with which attendees get promoted and how high they go in management. The study was done over about a ten-year period, and it found no correlation between success in leadership and program attendance. Some of the

P R O V E   I T

people that were in the highest positions and were the "rising stars" attended very few leadership development training programs.

It takes a lot of courage to challenge a program or strategy that management really believes in. Having the guts to ask for proof of success is very important. There should be very few things done on trust in an organization. Resources are tight, and it is important that each dollar and hour spent contributes to the mission or vision of the organization. *Proving it* means telling the emperor he is naked, even if your own head is at stake for your heresy. You may incur the wrath of senior management in the short run, but end up as a hero in the long run, by preventing your organization from continuing an ineffective strategy or program.

How to Prove It: Review What's Important

❏ *Don't shy away from challenging your organization's devotion to leadership development programs.* Many of these are just a feel-good waste of time: Top-level managers spend three days analyzing their personalities, work styles, and skills, but the organization doesn't really develop better leaders as a result.

❏ *Do try to emulate other companies that excel at leadership development.* This is a challenging task. But time devoted to researching companies like GE, which has a long track record of great succession planning, is better spent than on corporate boondoggles.

**P
R
O
V
E

I
T**

The Side Effects of Success

Have you ever read the literature that comes with any prescription drug you're taking? The list is enough to scare the hell out of you. Sure the drug will lower your blood pressure or cholesterol, but it may cause blindness, tumors, dizziness, water retention, headache, muscle soreness, stroke, heart palpitations, impotence, and a host of other maladies. You might be better off with high blood pressure than running the risk of all the side effects of this wonder drug. The drug company has to *prove* that the drug really does lower cholesterol—but at what cost? Success at one thing often causes problems in other areas. You finally make partner and get that million dollar paycheck you've worked for for twenty years, but find that your sixty-hour weeks are now eighty hours and your husband and kids don't even recognize you anymore.

Proving it means that you need to have data to show how successful your efforts are. Evaluating the success or failure of any strategy involves looking at key outcome measures, but it also involves looking at the impact on other relevant metrics. The concept called balanced scorecard, first proposed by Kaplan and Norton in a 1992 *Harvard Business Review* article is that you can't judge the success of an organization by looking solely at financial results. Many organizations have gotten into trouble in other areas like ethics, customer satisfaction, and employee morale while they were busy watching the bottom-line financial measures. One giant supermarket chain watched its financial results improve in a business known for thin margins. Then a strike by workers over health care benefits went on for over four months, and I wonder if that supermarket's management was monitoring the dissatisfaction of its employees with the precision and frequency with which it monitored its financial results.

Proving it means first identifying the primary one or two metrics that are supposed to get better if your strategy or program is to be judged successful. For example, a program might be designed to increase sales, lower costs, improve customer loyalty, or some other important outcome. Secondary measures also need to be identified that might be some of the "side effects" of your improvement effort. Increasing loyalty from the wrong customers might result in a decline in profits, as one of my clients found out. Their strategy really did work to increase loyalty, but the biggest increases came from their least profitable and biggest pain-in-the-butt accounts, so profits actually got worse. Another client implemented a successful strategy for improving employee morale and reducing turnover, but the star performers still left for other jobs and more of the deadwood stayed around longer.

Proving it means having the data to show that the desired goal or outcome of the effort has been achieved. What it also means is that you can't just look at one or two metrics. You need to identify a more *balanced* set of measures that could be affected in a positive or negative way by your intervention or strategy. An acquisition of a new company may immediately increase market share and top-line sales, which is great. You need to identify the other measures of performance that might be affected positively or negatively from this acquisition. Profits may or may not go up. Your brand image may be tarnished if the acquisition's quality is not as good as the parent company's. Other measures, such as overhead expense, communication, and customer satisfaction, might be affected as well.

Aspirin is clearly a wonder drug. It not only relieves headaches and other types of pain, it reduces the risk of heart attack and stroke, and it costs less than a penny a pill. However, even aspirin has side effects, like upset stomach and increased bruising. The side effects are clearly minor compared to the benefits of the drug, but they still need to be considered. The results of every strategy or program need to be examined very closely for their side effects, for there are side effects to every successful program, initiative, and product. *Proving*

P
R
O
V
E

I
T

the success of your efforts means showing that the benefits of improved performance far outweigh the costs and side effects.

How to Prove It: Review What's Important

❏ *Don't measure the success of any new program or initiative solely on one factor.* Doing so is misleading, because every action has multiple effects, and the "side effects" may be so deleterious that they outweigh the primary benefit of what you're trying to achieve.

❏ *Do consider a balanced set of measures for every new program you implement.* Look at the big picture to make sure your new approaches are really working on multiple levels, rather than one area improving at the expense of another.

**P
R
O
V
E

I
T**

Test Theories and Hypotheses

Organizations develop all these strange belief systems that are rarely supported with data. Wally got promoted to run the entire business unit in a company and moved from Chicago to Los Angles. When he arrived at the new job, one of his first executive decisions was to cancel casual dress for all employees and institute a new dress code that went back to suits, ties, and dresses, as he did at his plant in Chicago. Wally believed that business dress created a more professional atmosphere and encouraged greater productivity and professionalism. There was an outcry from employees who had always been able to dress in a casual manner. Wally's new policy meant spending hundreds of dollars on new clothes just to adhere to the new dress code. Wally was not a popular fellow when he first came to L.A.

I asked Wally about his decision and the effect it had on employee morale and their first impression of him, but he stuck to his guns about business dress creating a more professional work environment. I asked him if he had ever heard of a company called Microsoft, which was fairly successful with casual dress, and reminded him that even traditional IBM had gone more casual. I asked if he had ever read any research that showed a correlation between ties, panty hose, and employee productivity, and he admitted that he had not. Yet Wally stuck with the new policy, and employees got used to having to wear business clothes to work until Wally finally retired about five years later.

**P
R
O
V
E

I
T**

Wally was the boss, so he had the prerogative to make whatever policies he saw fit. The problem with practices like this is that they are not based on data, they are based on superstition. Wally's dress code is not more logical than the baseball pitcher who refuses to pitch without his lucky socks that he wore when he pitched a no-hitter. There are all sorts of superstitious policies and requirements in organizations that are not based on any hard data.

Proving it means having data to back up your business decisions, policies, practices, and requirements. What this means is that it is okay to come up with a theory or hypothesis, but that each one needs to be tested and proven valid or invalid before more resources are wasted on a hunch or superstition.

Greg was a sales manager for an accounting firm, and he liked his salespeople to report to him every day on who they called, who they visited, e-mails they wrote, and so forth. Greg spent an hour or two on the phone with each of his account managers each day, asking them to account for their time and coaching them on better approaches. Account managers dreaded these daily calls to Greg, and frequently made stuff up just so they sounded busy enough. Some learned to be very skilled liars because Greg probed for details on conversations, reactions of prospects, and so forth. Greg's hypothesis was that if you tightly control the behavior of account managers and control how they spend their time, they will bring in more business.

Well, the data said the opposite. Some of the most successful salespeople in the group did not call in to Greg to report on their activities, and left their cell phones unanswered when they knew it was Greg calling. Rather than spending an hour on the phone with their boss each day, the best account mangers spent their time building relationships with clients or prospects that resulted in more business.

It is important to come up with theories and hypotheses about ways in which you can improve performance. However, you need to keep in mind that many theories and hypotheses have been proven false with data. *Proving it* means having hard evidence that your actions produce results. Logic is not a good test because many logical actions sound great and have excellent surface credibility, but they fail to produce real results. Test each hypothesis and theory with hard data and that data will help you evolve and change your approaches to those that really do drive performance.

How to Prove It: Review What's Important

❏ *Don't simply adopt some new theory about how to work better without testing it first.* Too many managers have set-in-concrete ideas on how to work productively and efficiently, but many of these ideas have never been tested, and too many are actually just a waste of everyone's time. Don't implement new procedures just because you "think" they work.

❏ *Do test new ideas, and look at the hard data to see what works best.* If you can prove that something works everyone will buy into it, and your organization will be more productive and your employees will be happier.

P
R
O
V
E

I
T

Numbers Aren't Everything

The theme of this section of the book is about having the numbers or hard data to prove that the actions or strategies you've invested time in really work. Proof means evidence, charts, graphs, and statistics. Yet we all know that it is possible and fairly common for organizations to tell whatever story they want to tell by being selective in the numbers they choose to make their case. Most organizations don't overtly lie about their numbers; they find ways to put the proper spin on them and choose not to present statistics that make them look bad or don't further their cause.

Some things in an organization can actually be done on the basis of anecdotal data, gut feelings, past experience, or faith in a strategy or plan. An example might be safety training or technical training. It would be difficult and expensive to try to prove that your training reduced accidents or improved job performance enough to warrant the cost of the training. Back in the early 1980s, I helped big corporations conduct studies like this to prove their return on investment for training. Most of those corporations don't bother trying to prove that well-known strategies work. There are plenty of studies on the effectiveness of safety training, sales training, and a number of other strategies that organizations spend time and money on. Hence, not many organizations try to prove things that they already know work. Relying on someone else's research is perfectly acceptable in many cases. I don't need to read a paper on the efficacy of ibuprofen because it always seems to work for me.

Back in the 1980s, one giant company—one of the Dow 30 companies—used to have an entire department that conducted studies on the effectiveness of training and other HR initiatives. The department produced some compelling studies, which concluded that training is a good investment if it is focused on specific skills needed for good job performance. Well, there were no big surprises here, so the company eventually disbanded the evaluation department and put the staff to work designing and delivering training rather than conducting more studies to show that training really works.

Anecdotal or gut feeling data are often the most important to look at, particularly when you suspect that things just aren't right. Gina looked at the customer satisfaction numbers for her biggest account and they were exceptional, as they had been for the last few years. The client was giving the company high marks for all aspects of performance, but Gina still had a gut feeling that something was wrong. Her contacts did not return calls as promptly, were a little cold when interacting with her on the phone, and stiff when she saw them in person. She suspected that something was up, and sure enough, she found that a competitor was trying to lure away the business and that her customer was already working with the competitor on a limited basis. None of the numbers revealed that the account was in trouble, but other less quantifiable data turned out to be even more important.

The right measures can and should give you an indication that something is wrong or that things are okay, but since most measures are lagging indicators, by the time you get the report it is often too late. Just about anything can be quantified and measured, but a gut feeling is often more important than any formal statistics. Savvy managers won't simply accept that performance is good by looking at charts and graphs. Managers that *get it* don't spend all their time in meetings. Smart managers spend time with customers, front-line employees, suppliers, and other key stakeholders, to stay in touch with the business and get anecdotal data that they could not get from any meeting, chart, or Web site.

Proving the effectiveness of your approaches, programs, and strategies does mostly involve having hard data that shows results. If you don't have your own data, at least have studies conducted by others that prove that an approach really works. Beware if the

P
R
O
V
E

I
T

research is conducted by the same organization that is trying to sell you the program or approach, however. The other side of proving the success of your efforts is that your eyes and guts tell you the same things the numbers tell you. If the numbers look good but your instincts tell you to be worried, you should probably be worried. The key to being a good leader is to be analytical, but to also be observant and intuitive. *Proving it* means more than having the right numbers. It means convincing people to believe and trust your plans and strategies.

How to Prove It: Review What's Important

❑ ***Don't rely solely on charts, graphs, and statistics.*** Hard data is certainly good, and you should definitely keep track of your organization's performance by looking at the numbers. But remember that numbers alone don't tell the whole story of how you're doing.

❑ ***Do pay attention to your gut feelings and instincts regarding performance.*** These can be just as valuable as numbers and hard data—and sometimes more so. Make sure you make time to talk to your employees, customers, shareholders, and colleagues to solicit anecdotal information in addition to the statistical data.

PROVE IT

References

Bossidy, Larry, Charam, Ram, and Burck, Charles. *Execution—The Discipline of Getting Things Done*. New York: Crown Business, 2002.

Buckingham, Marcus, and David O Clifton. *Now, Discover Your Strengths*. New York: Free Press, 2001.

Buckingham, Marcus, and Curt Coffman. *First Break All the Rules—What the World's Greatest Managers Do Differently*. New York: Simon & Schuster, 1999.

Collins, Jim. *Good to Great—Why Some Companies Make the Leap . . . And Others Don't*. New York: HarperCollins, 2001.

Gilbert, Thomas. *Human Competence*. New York: McGraw-Hill, 1978.

Kaplan, Robert, and David Norton. *The Balanced Scorecard—Translating Strategy into Action*. Cambridge, MA: Harvard Business School Press, 1996.

Kawasaki, Guy, and Michele Moreno. *Rules for Revolutionaries—The Capitalist Manifesto for Creating and Marketing New Products and Services*. New York: HarperBusiness, 2000.

Page, Rick. *Hope Is Not a Strategy—The Six Keys to Winning the Complex Sale*. New York: McGraw-Hill, 2003.

Index

About the Author

Mark Graham Brown has been consulting with major corporations and government organizations on measuring and improving performance for the last 25 years. His clients include all branches of the U.S. Military, as well as many federal and state government organizations. Corporate clients include: Bose, Medtronic, Bank of America, Bechtel, Northrop Grumman, and Raytheon. He has had his own consulting practice since 1990. Prior to starting his own firm, he was a Principal in the Chicago firm of Svenson & Wallace, and was the manager of a group of consultants for Creative Universal in Detroit. In addition, he teaches public workshops on performance metrics in the U.S. and Europe for the Institute for Management Studies.

Mark is the author of the first and best selling book written on understanding the Baldrige Award criteria, which is currently in its 13th edition. He has authored many other books, including two on developing balanced scorecards: *Keeping Score—Using the Right Metrics to Drive World-Class Performance* (Productivity Press, 1996) and *Winning Score—How to Design and Implement Organizational Scorecards* (Productivity Press, 2000). Mark holds a master's degree in industrial psychology.